Time for Literacy Centers

How to Organize and Differentiate Instruction

Gretchen Owocki

HEINEMANN
Portsmouth, NH

Heinemann
A division of Reed Elsevier Inc.
361 Hanover Street
Portsmouth, NH 03801–3912
www.heinemann.com

Offices and agents throughout the world

Cataloging-in-Publication data is on file at the Library of Congress.
0-325-00731-4

Editor: Lois Bridges
Production: Vicki Kasabian
Cover design: Jenny Greenleaf
Typesetter: Publishers' Design and Production Services, Inc.
Manufacturing: Steve Bernier

Printed in the United States of America on acid-free paper
09 08 07 06 05 EB 1 2 3 4 5

*For David Owocki
and our little Emilia*

Acknowledgments   vii
Introduction   ix

CHAPTER **1**   Using Learning Principles to Guide Center-Based
Instruction   1

CHAPTER **2**   Using Literacy Goals to Plan for Centers   16

CHAPTER **3**   Organizing the Physical Environment for
Centers   31

CHAPTER **4**   Managing Center-Based Instruction   46

CHAPTER **5**   Differentiating the Instruction   69

CHAPTER **6**   The Centers   88

Bibliography   153
Index   157

I owe much gratitude to the dozens of early childhood teachers who have shown me the way to effective literacy centers. Special thanks to Nancy Biederman, Christian Bush, Sarah Coates, Christine Eaton, Charlene Gentry, Trish Hill, Barb Huston, Denise Ives, Curt Kiwak, Karen Kopacz, Carol Liss, and Kathy Meakins.

I also wish to thank the remarkable graduate students at Saginaw Valley State University, whose teaching and thinking stand with the best. Their work continually informs mine.

Finally, I wish to thank the crew at Heinemann for so skillfully doing what they do, with a special thanks to my astute and tranquil editor, Lois Bridges.

"How full of creative genius is the air in which these are generated!" Thoreau (1856) was making an observation about snow crystals, but he could easily have been making an observation about children. As we know of *both*, no two are alike.

Snow crystals differ from one another because they form in varying environments and because each is made up of millions of water molecules, some quite unusual. There is simply the slimmest of slim chances, in the whole lifetime of the universe, that any two snow crystals would ever end up the same. In turn, children's lives take shape in varying environments; each child is made up of millions of experiences, some quite unusual. There is simply no chance, in the whole lifetime of the universe, that any two children would ever end up the same; they would never end up knowing exactly the same things or learning in exactly the same ways.

Children differ. They come from families big and small and active and changing; from families with ideas about politics and schooling and religion and history; from families whose members spend their days growing strawberries, assembling cars, designing computer software, or caring for the elderly. They grow up in pretty, old neighborhoods, in wealthy new subdivisions, on impoverished dairy farms, in tiny barrio apartments. Their families' interests range from BMX racing and video gaming to reading books and watching television; from hockey and boxing to Guatemalan history and space science.

By the time they come to your classroom, even if they are only five or six years old, your students' experiences vary greatly, and this means that so, too, do their literacies. The creative genius that their families have used to make their way in the world has shaped very unique little individuals who walk down very different paths of learning. Some see themselves as literate; others think that reading and writing are for big kids and grown-ups. Some have begun to read a few words; others have begun to read all kinds of text. Some write in varied genres; others write only the words they are sure they can spell correctly. Some may be learning English as a second language. Perhaps one is learning English as a third language. Some boldly leave the classroom during the morning for special education services. Some cling to you and accidentally call you *Mom*.

How do today's teachers meet the literacy needs of a widely diverse set of learners? Effective teachers make use of literacy centers (Pressley, Rankin, and Yokoi 2000). A *literacy center* is an area of the classroom in which a set of literacy-related materials is arranged for collaborative exploration. Children working in centers use general activities and materials organized by the teacher—sometimes differentiated for individuals or groups—to set the direction and pace of their own activity. The teachers individualize and differentiate their instruction both on the spot and through preplanned teaching efforts.

You know that you can engage in center-based instruction, but how can you do it well? How can you do it in such a way that *all* of your students will be able to use centers to expand their literacy knowledge and so that *all* will use centers to deeply explore a wide range of content-related concepts? In this book, you will find ideas for organizing and implementing kindergarten through third-grade literacy centers and ideas for differentiating the instruction and experiences that occur there. Numerous examples from diverse classrooms are included. The information is appropriate for teachers trying out centers for the first time as well as for center veterans wishing to improve or expand on what they are doing already. In the chapters, you will find

- a set of learning principles that will help guide and enhance your center-based instruction

- a set of literacy goals for centers that is appropriate for consideration by kindergarten through third-grade teachers

- ideas for organizing the physical environment of the classroom for centers

- ideas for managing center-based instruction

- ideas for differentiating center-based literacy experiences and instruction

- plans for more than fifty literacy centers (most of which contain several activity ideas)

The content of this book is directly in line with the literacy goals and teaching practices endorsed by the National Association for the Education of Young

Children (NAEYC), the International Reading Association (IRA), and the National Council of Teachers of English (NCTE), which, importantly, inform many state curriculum frameworks. The book also provides information that is useful to schools and districts attempting to work thoughtfully with Reading First initiative guidelines. Specifically, those guidelines recommend that teachers provide instruction in *phonemic awareness, phonics, fluency, vocabulary,* and *comprehension.* The book addresses ways to support student development of these competencies (as well as other competencies, such as writing and book handling) in an integrated way, through developmentally appropriate experiences.

CHAPTER 1

Using Learning Principles to Guide Center-Based Instruction

A sun-browned boy with smudged hands and face trudged into Marie Ingle's classroom on the first day of school. He smelled of the things a child's day brings—red licorice, hard play, bicycle grease, and earth—and he appeared a little tired, as if he had already been through a full day of play. But his smile, with its dimple and chipped front tooth, was noticeably radiant.

The boy found his name tag on one of the desks and sat down without speaking. Ah, this was *Travis*. Marie had heard about Travis already. Travis had been held back after his first year of kindergarten. He would be receiving special pullout services this year. His speech would be difficult to understand. He might not have a warm coat for winter. He wouldn't talk much.

Centers Are a Place for All Learners

Throughout the year, Travis and Marie would find themselves watching the clock to be sure that Travis got to his speech and resource classes at the appropriate times. Although Travis wasn't the only child to leave the classroom during the day, he was the one to leave most often. Because he missed some instructional time with his classmates, he wasn't always familiar with the story characters they were joking about, the poems they were chanting, or the projects that had them "studying on" fairy tales, butterflies, magnetic forces, and community workers. With the still innocent candor of seven-year-olds, the other children sometimes asked, "Travis, do you go to speech so you can learn to talk right?" or "Is Travis smart, like we are?" Although his smile endured, the self-questioning and embarrassment that often crept into it showed the sting.

By late September, Marie had noticed that Travis' speech difficulties and learning disabilities (just *differences* in her eyes), in combination with his leaving the classroom, had begun to constrain his collaboration with other students. Travis had attained a "not capable" stigma among his peers that was beginning to negatively affect his classroom interactions as well as his view of himself as a learner.

But when center times began, they alleviated this. Centers, with their differentiated activities, experiences, and supports, have allowed Travis a view of himself as a first-rate learner, knowledgeable and capable just like the other students. As with all students, he can bring to centers his unique knowledge and his unique ways of listening, interpreting, understanding, and expressing, and he can use these in unfettered ways to support his learning.

Using Learning Principles to Guide Instruction

This chapter uses Travis' example, along with examples from some other children, to illustrate a set of *learning principles* (see Figure 1–1) that may be used to help shape your center-based instruction. Teachers instruct most effectively when they draw on a keen understanding of *how* children learn—or on learning *principles*—differentiating their approaches as they come to know individual students and their sociocultural contexts for living and growing (Bredekamp and Copple 1997). *Differentiating* refers to when teachers adjust

---

Learning Principles to Guide Center-Based Literacy Instruction

Meaningful learning . . .

- builds from a child's sociocultural experiences
- builds from a child's interests, tastes, and preferences
- progresses uniquely for each child
- occurs through child-directed talk and social collaboration
- is grounded in functional activity
- is the result of an active teacher within each child

Figure 1–1 *Learning Principles to Guide Center-Based Literacy Instruction*

and vary instruction, materials, activities, and learning environments in response to individual children's strengths and needs; it refers also to the choices that *children* make in environments that are appropriately set up for them to make some of their own learning decisions. In a differentiated setting, the depth, complexity, and nature of an experience regularly vary from child to child and from activity to activity.

As we consider the principles, you might wish to begin to think about how the centers in your classroom embody the characteristics of these principles and allow for differentiation to occur. A set of questions at the end of each section is provided to set a course for your reflections.

Sociocultural Experiences

The thermometer at the bank reads twenty-nine degrees, but with the snow flying horizontally, it feels much colder outside. It is almost dark. Travis and two of his younger sisters are on the sidewalk, playing with a sort of kite that they have assembled from a rope and a plastic grocery bag. One of the sisters is wearing Travis' army coat with the broken zipper. Travis wears only a sweatshirt.

When children—all children—come to us, they already have vast funds of knowledge (Moll and Greenberg 1990) and vast experience with all aspects of being. They have played, talked, discovered, created, cared, loved, and lived. They know well what their families and communities have taught them, and they know well how to make their way in their environments. *Meaningful learning builds from a child's sociocultural experiences*—from those intricate webs of knowledge, and those complex ways of thinking and feeling, that have amazingly been fashioned through just five or six or seven years.

Travis is one of the eldest in a family of many children. His life experiences, including those of being both an older and a younger brother, have given him skills and sensibilities that extend beyond what might be expected of a child so young. He skillfully plays and works with others in all kinds of situations. He creates elaborate treasures—such as kites and bicycle kickstands—from the simplest of materials. He is good at things involving money—counting, adding, subtracting, and shopping. He knows how to keep his thin sisters warm on a howling winter evening.

In the school setting, having opportunities to draw on such strengths gives Travis opportunities to grow in directions that are important for him. For example, his speech is difficult to understand, but during his carefully crafted center time, he works hard to use language that can be understood, and his peers work hard to understand him. They all know (perhaps without being consciously aware of it) that Travis' resourcefulness can extend activities in fun new directions, and in sticky situations, it can help keep things going. Sometimes, he lays his hand gently over that of another child and uses techniques learned in his speech class to slowly articulate how to play a game . . . or to tell the child that he is out of turn or out of line. Or he quietly listens to a child who is struggling with a concept, often related to math, and then softly explains his perspective. Often, these efforts involve repairing and clarifying his speech for the listener, as well as rephrasing to clarify his own thinking. When he recently demonstrated for the class how to make a kite, he made an utmost attempt at clarity, and his peers sat enthralled. When the follow-up center activity involved each child in writing instructions to remember what Travis had demonstrated, he became a resource whom the other children simply would *not* leave alone. Travis loved it.

With open-ended space, and encouragement, to use and share his sociocultural knowledge, Travis is developing his oral language, something that is much needed at this point in his development. But it isn't just language that he is developing as he interacts with peers in centers; a caring and broadly intelligent little human being is developing there, too. By showing others how to play games, make things, and think through math problems, Travis is expanding a *disarming* sensitivity to other human beings that has been nurtured in his home setting. By using his collaborative skills to participate in all kinds of problem-solving activities, he is expanding his knowledge about literacy, math, science, and art. From watching him work in centers, it has become clear that along with sensitivity and knowledge, Travis is developing a sense of *confidence* that is supporting his learning endeavors. Travis has much to offer to his learning community, and centers allow him to offer it.

Literacy centers provide many opportunities for teaching and learning to draw from beyond the classroom walls. In addition to Travis' strengths, the students in Marie's classroom bring knowledge about farming, growing vegetables, making ice cream, and caring for pets; they know about games, toys, cartoons, songs, religion, health care, and family traditions. With these pieces of world knowledge come the literacies that are associated with them: with family traditions there are stories, recipes, letters, and crafts; with toys, there are adventures, advertisements, packages, and logos; with ice cream there are recipes, food packages, grocery lists, and words to describe flavors; and so forth. The opportunity for children to share their experiences with these literacies provides an important arena for Marie and all of the children to grow—both as rounded human beings and as literate individuals.

Sociocultural Experiences: You Reflect

A sociocultural theory of learning recognizes that children's life experiences provide a foundation from which all new learning occurs. Sociocultural theories promote "multiple ways of thinking and multiple definitions of important knowledge; they support a wide range of cultural perspectives and practices in the school curriculum; and they justify using social interaction as the primary medium of instruction" (Oakes and Lipton 2003, 85). As you reflect on the centers in your classroom, ask yourself how a sociocultural theory of learning is embodied in the activity that takes place there. The following questions may help guide your planning:

- What am I learning about each of my students' sociocultural knowledge and experience? Am I able to spontaneously list at least one strength of each child in my classroom?

- What ways of using language and literacy are connected with my students' sociocultural knowledge?

- How do I use what I know about my students' sociocultural experiences to help shape and differentiate center activities?

- How could I work with family members so that they might contribute to classroom sharing of sociocultural knowledge and experiences?

Interests, Tastes, and Preferences

Ryan, a first grader in Christian Bush's classroom, has been dubbed *class scientist*. At center time one day, as the other children rotate from center to center, he stays on the floor with a book that he has borrowed from Christian. He is taking notes so that he will remember how to conduct an experiment that he wants to try at home.

The next principle to consider as you implement centers is that *meaningful learning builds from a child's interests, tastes, and preferences*. Ryan loves science. He has already demonstrated for the class one experiment from home. He plans to do more. His center activity today has him reading for information, synthesizing the information, and preparing to take his ideas home to share with his family. He does this work in a big-book center in which he has chosen the book and he has chosen the activity. As his teacher, Christian, observes him, she reflects: "When they do their own thing, it's so much more meaningful, and they learn so much more, than when I try to control the activities." Ryan has indicated to Christian that he wants to know more about fossils and has concluded that they take "ten or three days" to form. When Christian finds just the right book on fossils, I have no doubt that Ryan will wrap himself in it for a full center period, with a focus so intense that he will, again, seem oblivious to the activity around him.

When children are *interested* in material, they are most likely to engage with it in a way that moves them into new frontiers of understanding (Dewey 1897). Just think of the way that your own students become focused when they are writing or reading about topics that interest them: reading on the Internet to find the answer to a pertinent question; working through a word puzzle that they enjoy; or waiting with excitement to find out how a book ends. Their motivation to use and problem solve written language is high because there is an urge to know more; an urge to express an idea; something unsolved; something unstated. As you plan center activities, and as you think about how to differentiate children's experiences within them, keep in mind that the curiosity, tension, and motivation that drive new language learning arise from interesting, appealing content. For *each* child, interest moves learning forward.

Interest is important not only from a *learning* perspective but also from an *assessment* perspective. When interest is high, teachers are best able to see what children are capable of doing and what they are capable of learning next (Dewey 1897). For example, Marie's student Travis is well known for appreciating bookshelf humor. Although he is just beginning to make sense of decoding processes, during center time, he regularly huddles in the book corner, reading aloud—and sounding quite fluent—with two other boys. Following Michael's lead, the three children read chorally in their husky little whisper voices, interrupted only by Travis' laughter, so contagious that it often starts the other two giggling—loudly! Even though Marie has read many of these books to the class five or six times, the boys' taste for humor inspires them to read them again and again.

Their *interest* in the material draws their attention to comprehending and decoding print that would typically be considered above their reading levels. Importantly, observing the boys at this time gives Marie information about the kinds of text that will stretch their motivation and thinking and will therefore make sense to use for comprehension and decoding instruction. Because centers value children's unique tastes and preferences, they create opportunities for children to show what they are able to do when they have pushed themselves to the edge of their capabilities.

Interests, Tastes, and Preferences: You Reflect

Coming to know children's interests is important to instruction. It is only through observation of each child's interests that teachers can "enter into the child's life and see what it is ready for, and upon what material it could work most readily and fruitfully" (Dewey 1897, 79). Considering questions such as the following will support your planning as you work to incorporate children's interests into your centers:

■ What am I learning about each of my students' interests? Am I able to spontaneously list at least one interest for each child in my classroom?

■ What literacies are connected to these interests?

■ How do I use what I know about my students' interests to help shape and differentiate center activities? Are all of the students included in this process?

■ What assessment do I do as children connect with high-interest topics and material?

Individual Learning Progress

Jerome, a first grader, is interviewing his classmate Max for a biography he is writing. "Where did you grow up?" Jerome asks.

"Swan Creek," Max responds. Then, he speaks slowly, giving Jerome time to spell: "Growed . . . up . . . in . . . Swan . . . Creek."

The third principle to consider as you implement centers is that *meaningful learning progresses uniquely for each child*. To fully make use of this principle, it is important to recognize that literacy *progress* is not linear; instead, literacy develops along several paths all at once. For example, the first graders in the vignette are working on a simple biography, but just think about all of the literacy paths along which they must be developing in order to accomplish this task. They must consider how the text in a biography is *organized*, the kinds of *information* that biographies contain, how to write in the *third person*, how to structure *sentences*, how to *punctuate*, how to *spell*, and how to communicate meaningfully with an *audience*. As children learn to read and write, they progress along numerous paths all at once, and, central to this principle, they follow each path *at their own paces, using their own ways of knowing.*

At the time of writing the biography, both Max and Jerome had a good sense of how biographies are organized and of the information that they ought to contain. But these children *differed in their understandings* of how to structure sentences, punctuate, spell, and communicate with a distant audience. They also *differed in their approaches* to learning new things. For Max, writing and talk seemed to be ideal ways to develop and express his knowledge, but for Jerome, drawings seemed more cardinal.

As John Dewey noted more than a hundred years ago, in order to meet children's complex and diverse needs, the "child's own instincts and powers [must] furnish the material and give the starting point for all education" (1897, 77). Current research confirms this. A recent study of first-grade classrooms shows that the most *effective* literacy teachers differentiate their instruction by providing a variety of activities—"they do not give everyone in the class the same task to do; rather, they individualize assignments. Sometimes this means students are doing very different things at the same time, sometimes it means they are doing the same thing with adjustments on a student-by-student basis" (Pressley et al. 2001, 221). Similar findings from another recent study show that in *exemplary* classrooms, it is more common for students to be working at similar but unique tasks than to find all students doing exactly the same thing (Allington 2002). Planned sensitivity to individual students is the norm in effective primary classrooms, with the most effective teachers assessing children's *knowledge* and *ways of knowing* and adjusting their instruction accordingly (Allington 2002; Pressley et al. 2001; Pressley, Rankin, and Yokoi 2000).

Individual Learning Progress: You Reflect

Implementing centers effectively requires keeping in mind that children know different things *and* they have different ways of knowing. All children do not respond well to the same activities or the same types of instruction. Therefore, centers must be a place for differentiation. Teachers differentiate by varying instructional support, materials, and activities. Children differentiate by making many of their own choices. Differentiation ensures that learning time is efficiently spent, rather than aimed at what most children in the classroom might want or need. As you plan centers, you may wish to consider the following questions:

■ What am I learning about each of my students' literacy knowledge?

- How am I setting up center activities to allow for individual progress?

- What adaptations do I make for individual students?

- How do centers allow for different approaches to learning the same concept?

Talk and Social Collaboration

Shaun, a kindergartner, is writing a retelling of *The Three Little Pigs*. "How do you write *pigs?*" she asks Danitra.

"You know how to write *pigs*. It's right up there [on the word wall]!"

Shaun copies the word and then draws a pig, counting aloud as she places five fingers on each hoof. Later, as she orally retells, she realizes what her drawing is missing: "The wolf blew the house . . . *straw* house," she says, and then she pauses to draw straw on the house.

The next principle to consider as you teach with centers is that *meaningful learning occurs through child-directed talk and social collaboration*. Talk is the primary symbol system through which children construct knowledge about the world. It is through talk that children come face-to-face with their ideas, making them into something concrete—something that they can refine, contemplate, shape, and act on (Lindfors 1991). And it is through talk that children think and construct knowledge together and prompt one another to consider ideas and concepts a step beyond what they might consider on their own. When children are in charge of the talking, they have opportunities to tailor the conversation to meet *their* particular needs.

The vignette illustrates this important role that talk plays in guiding thinking and learning. Shaun uses *self-talk* to manage her spelling of words, her counting of objects, her drawing, and her rethinking of the story. Children use self-talk as a tool to accomplish tasks that would be otherwise too difficult to achieve, with the amount of talk increasing as the action becomes more challenging and complex (Vygotsky 1978).

The social, collaborative part of Shaun's talk is important, too. In the vignette, she first receives information from Danitra about how to find a spelling for a word. Then later, as they retell together, they notice some things that are missing from the illustration. In collaboration, Shaun moves her thinking a step past where she would likely have moved on her own.

Research in elementary classrooms shows that exemplary literacy teachers encourage lots of talk, both among children and among children and teachers. High-quality talk is purposeful and connected to curricular topics, but it is *conversational* rather than characterized by teachers doing all of the asking and evaluating and children doing all of the responding (Allington 2002).

Under what conditions do children engage in such high-quality talk? A review of studies in the field of early literacy shows that knowledge-enhancing classroom talk occurs as children encounter challenging concepts; have control over the direction of their explorations; read and write about topics they find meaningful; and engage in social play (Whitmore et al. 2004). With thoughtful planning, center-based instruction makes rich and educative talk possible.

Talk and Social Collaboration: You Reflect

Setting up a rich environment for talk and collaboration allows children to gain control over the literacy concepts and practices that are currently relevant to *them*. The following questions will help you plan centers that are characterized by quality talk and collaboration:

- What are my students talking about as they work in centers?

- Are center activities challenging and intriguing enough to inspire (and require) both self-talk and social talk?

- Do the children use talk in a way that helps them experience language or consider concepts that are just beyond what they might consider on their own? Is this happening for *all* of the children? If not, what kinds of differentiation might help?

Meaningful, Functional Activity

Tionna and her third-grade classmates have spent the past weeks using center time to study issues related to pollution. For her inquiry project, Tionna is gathering information to write a report that exposes information about beach closings in the local area and across the United States. At the computer center, she printed an article from *www.kidsnewsroom.org*. In the independent reading center, she highlighted information from it to include in her report. Now in the author center, she is drawing a diagram of a cruise ship dumping sewage near a beach.

The next principle to consider as you implement centers is that *meaningful literacy learning is grounded in functional activity*. Children learn by interacting with the knowledge of their culture *as it is being used* (Dewey 1897). Just as they learn to talk by talking, to swim by actually swimming, and to follow a recipe by actually cooking, they learn to read and write by using reading and writing to serve authentic purposes (Goodman and Goodman 1990). Therefore, "teaching should be organized in such a way that reading and writing are necessary for something" (Vygotsky 1978, 117).

As Tionna works on her project, reading and writing are necessary for learning and reporting about water pollution. Tionna uses reading and writing to serve real goals. Through the process she is developing her knowledge in all areas of the language arts. The International Reading Association (1998) defines the language arts to include reading, writing, listening, speaking, viewing, and visually representing and recommends that children be provided with opportunities to integrate experiences across these categories. Integration allows one language art to inform the development of the others. For example, *viewing* can help children learn to *visually represent*; learning about text structures through *writing* can support children's *reading*. However, integration "is not simply using one of the language arts to support another . . . , but the coordinated instruction of some combination of the major language processes as tools to achieve a learning goal" (Gavelek et al. 2000, 590). Meaningful learning and teaching draw on the language arts *to achieve real goals*.

The plan in Figure 1–2 provides an example of a set of centers that draws on all of the language arts to support children's understandings of science content. Figure 1–3 provides a blank form that may be used for your own integrated planning.

Meaningful, Functional Activity: You Reflect

Ultimately, an integrated, center-based approach is steeped in functional activity that supports children's development of all of the language arts. The following questions will help you to plan for functional uses of written language in integrated centers.

- How are the language arts being used to achieve real learning goals? Do these goals seem relevant to each child in my classroom? If not, what kinds of differentiation might help?

- What steps can I take to integrate language and literacy goals with content inquiries?

Planning Form for Literacy Centers

Literacy Focus: __reading nonfiction; retelling/reporting information__

Content Focus: __endangered species__   Dates: __November 5–23__

Center	Activities	Read	Write	Listen	Speak	View	Vis. Rep.	Content Areas
Reading and Vocabulary	Read your choice of endangered species books. Record on note cards interesting vocabulary. Draw and write a definition. Place alphabetically in the class word file.	x	x			x	x	• Science
Writing and Vocabulary	Write and illustrate a page for our class book *Our New Understandings About Endangered Species.*		x			x		• Science
Computer	With a partner, read (from two specified websites) to find answers to your endangered species questions. Add new questions to the list.	x	x	x	x	x		• Science
Observation	View a video and record information about the habitats of endangered species.		x	x		x		• Science
Play	Construct a sanctuary for endangered animals.			x	x		x	• Science • Social Studies
Home Connections	Discuss homework: What endangered or extinct animals does your family know about? Graph information to identify most known.			x	x		x	• Science • Math
Poetry	Read and write poetry—focus on free verse. Focus on the natural environment.	x	x					• Science
Retelling	With a partner, fill out a graphic organizer to use for sharing (with whole class) information from one book (students choose from four designated books).	x	x	x	x	x	x	• Science
Words	With group, make words (at least four letters) out of a big word: *endangered, habitats,* or *environment.*		x		x	x		—

Figure 1–2 *Planning Form for Literacy Centers*

Figure 1–3 *Planning Form for Literacy Centers*

Planning Form for Literacy Centers

Literacy Focus: _____

Content Focus: _____ Dates: _____

Center	Activities	Language Arts						Content Areas
		Read	Write	Listen	Speak	View	Vis. Rep.	

© 2005 Gretchen Owocki from *Time for Literacy Centers*. Portsmouth, NH: Heinemann.

The Teacher Within

Twelve-month-old Emilia finds a canister containing two spice bottles. She smiles at her dad, seeming to say, "Something new!" She lifts the lid, replaces it, and then scratches its bumpy ridges. She smiles again at her dad. She looks inside the canister and touches one of the bottles before pulling it out. She puts each bottle in her mouth, then shakes one, watching the ingredients inside. She puts the bottles back in the canister and pulls them out again.

The final principle to consider as you implement centers is that *meaningful learning is the result of the active teacher that resides within every child*. Little Emilia illustrates a characteristic typical of all children: all are *wired* to figure out how the world works—to assume agency for their learning and to do it every chance they get. Why do young children touch everything, taste everything, put a finger into everything, and open everything? Why do they shake and pat things, pull and push them, stack and tumble them, climb them and jump off? Why do they seem driven to talk and listen and share their experiences with others? Because human nature tells them to explore and discover the world—and all of the important values and practices within it. Children *will* discover, because that's what they're cut out to do, and literacy is a part of what they will discover because of its value within our culture.

Sometimes teachers think of literacy centers as places for children to only *practice* skills and strategies that have been taught rather than places to develop significant new competencies. But that's not how learning works. Developmental psychologists have taught us that children learn by developing a personal working model (or set of hypotheses) for how everything in their worlds works, including written language. Any time a thought, an object, an event, or another person challenges or nudges that model, the child adjusts it to account for the new information (Bredekamp and Copple 1997; Ferreiro and Teberosky 1982; Piaget 1952). Therefore, children *learn* in any environment that allows them to engage with new ideas or materials or that prompts them into new ways of thinking. Children can do much more than *practice* in centers. They can actually develop new competencies.

Before children can do intelligent work in centers, they need a learning environment that values who they are and that values their uniqueness. The learning principles described in this chapter center around valuing each child's sociocultural experiences and interests, each child's unique knowledge, and each child's unique ways of thinking and learning. Effective center-based teaching—teaching that differentiates—involves starting with a rich, choice-filled environment and then kidwatching to find ways to ensure that you are capitalizing on individual strengths and meeting individual needs.

The Teacher Within: You Reflect

Given a rich and talk-filled environment, children do substantial *new* learning as their inner teachers sort out all of the new ideas they encounter and generate. Therefore, in developmentally appropriate classrooms, teachers "provide many opportunities for children to plan, anticipate, reflect on, and revisit their own learning experiences. They engage children in discussion and representation activities (such as writing, drawing, or constructing models) to help children refine their own concepts and thinking and help themselves understand children's thinking" (Bredekamp and Copple 1997, 167). In other words, developmentally appropriate teachers give children's inner teachers the freedom to do their own teaching. The following questions will help you reflect on the inner teaching in your classroom and plan your centers accordingly.

- What freedom do my students have to test *their* hypotheses and refine their *own* concepts about written language?

- What conditions seem to best foster children's hypothesis testing, or the activity of their inner teachers? How do these conditions *differ* among students?

CHAPTER 2

Using Literacy Goals to Plan for Centers

In a United States survey of primary teachers nominated as effective in promoting literacy, 100 percent of the kindergarten teachers, 85 percent of the first-grade teachers, and 73 percent of the second-grade teachers reported using literacy centers as part of their literacy instruction (Pressley, Rankin, and Yokoi 2000). In today's classrooms, effective teachers are creating environments in which children are spending quality school time exploring literacy without a teacher's immediate presence. In fact, young children may spend from one to two hours per day in such a setting. Given this situation, it is clear that "instruction away from the teacher needs to be as powerful as instruction with the teacher" (Ford and Opitz 2002, 719).

Purposeful planning with attention to *literacy goals* provides a foundation for such instruction. Literacy goals provide a base from which to plan and a beginning framework for observing children's growth. Figure 2–1 presents a set of general literacy goals that may be used as a starting point to shape your center-based literacy activities.

The goals are drawn from a wide body of research on language and literacy, as well as from recommendations from the National Association for the Education of Young Children, the International Reading Association, and the National Council of Teachers of English. Because these organizations typically inform state and district curriculum frameworks, it is likely that they will connect in many ways with the goals that you are already working toward. As a point of caution, keep in mind that any time you work with a set of goals or standards, it is important to reflect on how well they are helping you support meaningful learning for *your* students. If you focus only on how well students are achieving the goals, you may miss opportunities to capitalize on the multi-

---

Literacy Goals to Develop Through Centers

- an expanding sense of language and literacy as sociocultural practices
- book-handling and book-sharing knowledge
- reading comprehension and meaning-making strategies
- knowledge that supports word reading and spelling
- reading fluency
- expanded uses of and knowledge about writing
- vocabulary

Figure 2–1 *Literacy Goals to Develop Through Centers*

ple uses of language and literacy that your students are already demonstrating, and your teaching may fail to build on their actual competencies.

Tip for Differentiation

As you work with literacy goals, keep in mind that the specifics never look the same for any two children. For *each* child, the ultimate aim is to expand and extend what he or she already knows. Differentiation is about giving children supportive opportunities to grow from where they are today. To differentiate effectively, keep yourself open to observing what each student knows and can do and to planning in response to *the children's* strengths and needs.

Goal 1: Language and Literacy as Sociocultural Practices

An overarching goal for all children as they participate in centers is that they will expand their uses of language and literacy as *sociocultural practices*. From a teaching perspective, this goal refers not as much to instructing in the *specifics* of reading or writing as to providing children with opportunities to expand the ways in which they *use* reading, writing, and even talk to construct and express knowledge in various settings. For example, *reading* is one thing, but accurately following a set of written instructions to conduct an experiment, or finding and tripling a recipe for strawberry pudding, is another. *Writing* is one thing, but sending a letter to the newspaper to protest aerial wolf hunting, or making notes to plan a birthday party, is another. *Talking* is one thing, but using a specialized discourse to play as an emergency room worker or to express curiosity about the hatching of a nest of robin eggs is another. The first goal for children participating in literacy centers is that they will expand their uses of language, both written and oral, to serve multiple authentic purposes, including purposes related to school learning.

You can support this goal by ensuring that centers provide many opportunities for children to use the language arts as tools for achieving real purposes. If currently you operate centers that do not support this, a little adjustment may be all that is needed. For example, if *phonics knowledge* is a goal, but you have children filling in blanks on worksheets to achieve it, why not instead have them do some real writing? Filling in blanks just shows what children know *already*. Real writing creates a meaningful context that prompts *new* discoveries about phonics and, at the same time, about how to use writing to meet real goals. Or if *legible handwriting* is a goal, but you have students writing strings of letters to achieve it, why not instead have them compose a letter that they could really send to someone—or have them create *any* document that they would actually want to share with someone? Certainly a real audience for a real piece of writing would inspire neat writing and, maybe more important, would help your students develop understandings about how to use writing as a tool for learning and living. Exploring authentic uses of written language provides the context for children to develop all of the other competencies (goals) described in this chapter.

Tip for Differentiation

When you are setting up your centers, include some sort of *family connection* center in which children regularly have opportunities to share their real-life literacies. For example, you could arrange for a child or family member to demonstrate how to do something (make a kite, coffee-can ice cream, or a horsehair basket) or to bring in a set of materials (such as those used to care for a baby in the family). Children could explore the topic in the center all week. They could browse materials, read related literature (recipes, instructions, stories), and write texts ranging from instructions, to how they felt about the experience, to a thank-you note to the person who brought in the project.

Goal 2: Book-Handling and Book-Sharing Competencies

Along with sociocultural knowledge, you will want your literacy centers to be a place for children to develop a broad range of book-handling and book-sharing competencies. Figure 2–2 lists a set of key competencies that may be promoted (and assessed) through centers. These competencies should be developed or developing by the end of the kindergarten year, but children should continue to expand them throughout the early childhood years.

To promote well-rounded book handling and sharing, center activities must engage children socially in all kinds of book reading—fiction, nonfiction, and poetry—and must provide structured avenues for them to discuss what they have read. If book handling and sharing are to thrive, it also helps to ensure that the books are appealing to the children so that they have *reason* to dig in, think, and discuss.

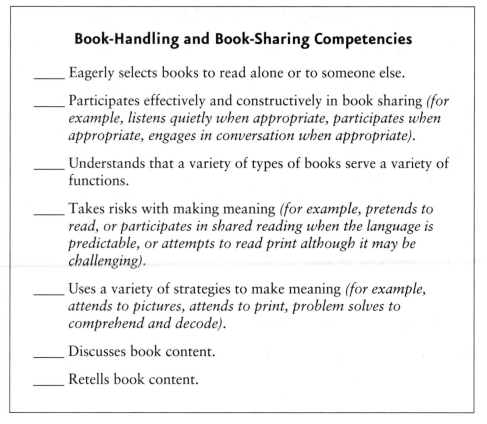

Book-Handling and Book-Sharing Competencies

_____ Eagerly selects books to read alone or to someone else.

_____ Participates effectively and constructively in book sharing *(for example, listens quietly when appropriate, participates when appropriate, engages in conversation when appropriate)*.

_____ Understands that a variety of types of books serve a variety of functions.

_____ Takes risks with making meaning *(for example, pretends to read, or participates in shared reading when the language is predictable, or attempts to read print although it may be challenging)*.

_____ Uses a variety of strategies to make meaning *(for example, attends to pictures, attends to print, problem solves to comprehend and decode)*.

_____ Discusses book content.

_____ Retells book content.

Figure 2–2 *Book-Handling and Book-Sharing Competencies*

Tip for Differentiation

During the early days of centers, watch children as they handle and
share books to see what they need from you. Keep an eye out for
children who may not have spent much time with books before
coming to school or who do not show much interest in reading. Some
children will need to be individually enticed into books with content
and conversation that are highly appealing to them. Some may need
specific prompts to get started discussing books. Some may need an
adult to sit with them at first, to help them learn to build meaning
across the pages of a book. A meaningful enculturation into book
handling and sharing sometimes takes a differentiated approach on
the teacher's part, but this is worth the effort because it provides a
strong foundation for all future learning.

Goal 3: Comprehension Strategies

Another goal for centers is that they will support children's development of
reading and listening comprehension strategies. *Comprehension strategies* are
what readers (and listeners) use to understand, think about, and communicate
about what has been read. Ultimately, readers use a range of strategies before,
during, and after any given reading event, flexibly emphasizing the ones most
needed to suit their purposes.

Figure 2–3 lists a set of comprehension strategies that may be encouraged
(and assessed) as children listen and read during center time. The strategies
should be applied as children engage with multiple genres, including fiction,
nonfiction, poetry, and computer media.

Successful teaching practices found to foster comprehension (and reading
development in general) include

- encouraging extensive reading

- making available a variety of texts (from a variety of genres) that appeal
  to students' interests

- encouraging reading for real reasons

Comprehension Strategies

____ Predicts and infers.
    What will come next?
    What does this mean?

____ Sets purposes and uses them to meet reading goals.
    Why am I reading?
    To what should I pay attention in order to meet my goals?

____ Monitors understandings.
    What is happening in the text?
    If I don't understand, what can I do?
    What questions do I have?

____ Uses personal knowledge and experience to inform the reading.
    *What from my experience or previous reading helps me
      connect with or understand this text?*
    What does this text make me visualize or see in my mind?

____ Uses text structures and formats as part of meaning making.
    How is the text formatted?
    How is the language organized?

____ Retells, summarizes, and synthesizes.
    What have I just read?

____ Evaluates.
    What do I think of this?
    Why did the author write this?

Figure 2–3 *Comprehension Strategies*

- providing students with opportunities to explore strategies that have been modeled and taught by the teacher

- observing students as they read and talking with them about their reading strategies; using what is learned to provide instruction that connects with student strengths and needs

- providing opportunities for students to respond to literature (Barton and Sawyer 2003; Owocki 2003; Pressley 2000; Taylor et al. 2000)

As you design and evaluate your reading and listening centers, make it a practice to think through criteria such as these.

Students most readily develop comprehension strategies when the material they are reading is of personal interest or connected with their experiences. Therefore, offer many opportunities for them to choose the literature they will read during center time. When *you* select the literature, look for books that connect with their interests and experiences as well as with the content area concepts that they are learning about in your classroom. When possible, allow English language and bilingual learners to read material in their stronger languages. Comprehension strategies and content knowledge that develop through reading and discussing in one language will transfer to the other language.

Goal 4: Knowledge That Supports Word Reading and Spelling

Along with book handling and comprehension, another goal is that centers will support children's development of word reading and spelling. Figure 2–4 shows four related areas of competency that centers may be designed to support. A description of each competency follows.

Alphabet Knowledge

Alphabet knowledge refers to understandings about the physical features (how letters look) and the functions (how letters are used) of the alphabet. Literacy centers aimed at fostering alphabet knowledge support children in writing let-

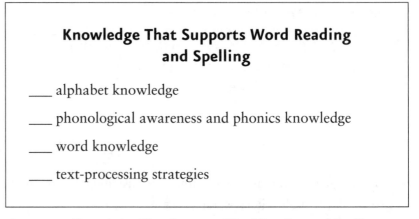

Knowledge That Supports Word Reading and Spelling

____ alphabet knowledge

____ phonological awareness and phonics knowledge

____ word knowledge

____ text-processing strategies

Figure 2–4 *Knowledge That Supports Word Reading and Spelling*

ters (or approximations) to represent meaning and in identifying and talking about letters as they appear in real contexts (such as books, names, environmental print, and games).

Although knowledge of the alphabet is a foundation for learning to write and read, children need not know all of the letters in order to begin to do either. For example, many children begin *writing* using only invented symbols or just a few letters—often those found in their names. Similarly, many children begin *reading* starting with family members' names or store names, even though they would not be able to identify every letter in those words. Using meaningful literacy experiences to talk about the alphabet is an important way to support children's development.

Tip for Differentiation

Connect alphabet learning with each child's life. If you teach kindergarten, arrange for each student to bring in one piece of environmental print that he or she can read (such as a toy logo, a book cover, or part of a cereal box). Place the pieces in a center and encourage children to read them to each other, to copy the ones that they can read, and to talk about the letters in the words.

Phonological Awareness and Phonics Knowledge

Phonological awareness refers to the ability to identify and analyze sound units (words, syllables, onsets, rimes, and phonemes) as they occur in *spoken* language. *Phonics knowledge* refers to understandings about the relationships between sound units and the *letters and spellings* that represent those units.

Although the term *phonological awareness* refers strictly to spoken language, current research indicates that children should be taught to use actual print *as* they learn to segment and blend the sound units in spoken words (National Reading Panel 2000). In other words, they should be encouraged to develop phonics knowledge and phonological awareness at the same time. In center-based settings, this typically happens through activities such as writing and shared writing, reading and shared reading, and engaging in word study. As you assess children's knowledge, keep in mind that their understandings may more easily reveal themselves *implicitly* than explicitly. That is, they may be able to *use* certain knowledge as they read or write but be unable to consciously articulate what they know.

Tip for Differentiation

Avoid letter-of-the-week programs. They are not necessary, and for many children, they are not helpful. Some children will already know the letter and will already be using it in their writing and reading. Some will find it difficult to connect letters primarily studied in isolation with real uses of reading and writing. And all children need more than one letter per week to write and read.

Instead of teaching one letter per week, individualize your instruction and focus on helping children develop the letters and sounds that they actually need as they write and read. There is no scientific evidence that studying one letter per week, in some special order, works better than focusing on letters and sounds as they are connected to meaningful reading and writing.

Word Knowledge

As children (even very young ones) are developing phonological awareness and phonics knowledge, teachers should also encourage their development of quick familiarity with high-frequency words (words regularly used in their reading or writing.) A reader's *sight word vocabulary* (developed through wide reading) refers to the words the reader can instantly recognize (because she has seen them often). Having a large sight word vocabulary helps children become fluent readers (Osborn, Lehr, and Hiebert 2004).

Key phonological, phonics, and word-related concepts for young children to develop are synthesized in Figure 2–5.

Text-Processing Strategies

Text-processing strategies refer to the efforts in which readers engage as they decode *connected* text, such as that in a book or a magazine. In the previous section I discussed the importance of children developing phonics and word knowledge; this knowledge is essential to proficient reading. However, text processing involves much more than identifying words.

The text processing of proficient readers is characterized by a continual monitoring of meaning. As they read, proficient readers continually think ahead, using what they know about language structure and meaning to anticipate what is coming next. So, if they come to text that reads, *The dog*

Phonological Awareness, Phonics Knowledge, and Word Knowledge	
Competency	*Examples and Explanations*
Phonological Awareness	
Identify rhyming words and *supply* rhymes for words.	• Identification: *Ship* rhymes with *dip*, but not with *wave*. • Supply: *Ship* rhymes with _____. [Child supplies word.]
Orally *segment* a word into sound units. (Children use this competency to help spell words.)	• Syllables: *shipping* into /ship/ /ping/ • Onsets and Rimes: *ship* into /sh/ /ip/ • Phonemes: *ship* into /sh/ /i/ /p/
Orally *blend* a word's sound units. (Children use this competency to help decode words.)	• Syllables: /ship/ /ping/ into *shipping* • Onsets and Rimes: /sh/ /ip/ into *ship* • Phonemes: /sh/ /i/ /p/ into *ship*
Phonics Knowledge	
Knowledge of letter-sound associations	Knowledge of the sound(s) that individual letters and letter patterns make
Word analysis strategies	Attending to the sounds associated with letters, letter combinations, and word parts and *blending* them together to read words or *segmenting* them to write words
Word Knowledge	
Knowledge of individual words	Ability to automatically recognize and write an increasing number of words

Figure 2–5 *Phonological Awareness, Phonics Knowledge, and Word Knowledge*

chewed the _____, they can reasonably predict that the missing word is a noun and something that a dog might chew. Predicting makes word identification easier, and interestingly, predicting is why readers sometimes make miscues like *The dog chewed the* **bone** for text that actually reads, *The dog chewed the* **board**. Smart predictions often lead to smart miscues!

When good readers lose meaning (*The dog chewed the **broke***), they realize it and use language structure and meaning to cross-check to get back on track. A cross-check involves thinking almost simultaneously along three lines: "Does that sound right [language structure]? Does it make sense [meaning]? Let me look more closely at the word." The text-processing strategies listed in Figure 2–6 (adapted from Owocki and Goodman 2002) may be encouraged as students read during center time.

Text-processing strategies develop as children read (and are supported in reading) actual text—text that is predictable and appropriately challenging. Text that is overly simplified or made "decodable" in order to emphasize phonics concepts (such as *Rat is fat and Cat is fat . . .*) may make reading more difficult than it needs to be because the text becomes less predictable and sensible.

Tip for Differentiation

To understand the different kinds of support that individual children need with word identification and text processing, make it a practice to regularly document their miscues or to take running records. For small-group strategy instruction, group children together who have similar miscue patterns.

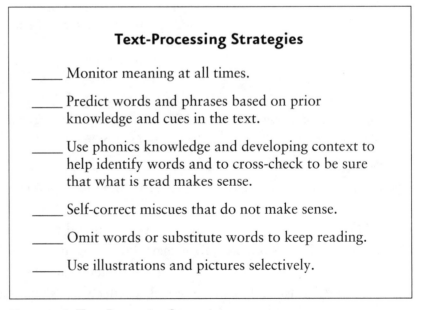

Text-Processing Strategies

_____ Monitor meaning at all times.

_____ Predict words and phrases based on prior knowledge and cues in the text.

_____ Use phonics knowledge and developing context to help identify words and to cross-check to be sure that what is read makes sense.

_____ Self-correct miscues that do not make sense.

_____ Omit words or substitute words to keep reading.

_____ Use illustrations and pictures selectively.

Figure 2–6 *Text-Processing Strategies*

Goal 5: Reading Fluency

Reading fluency is another competency that centers can be designed to support. *Fluency* is a term used to describe the reading of text in logical phrases, with meaningful intonation. Fluent readers typically decode with relative ease and accuracy, at a reasonably quick pace, automatically recognizing a number of words. Fluency is considered important because it allows readers to focus their attention on comprehending rather than on decoding (Adams 1990; Allington 2001; LaBerge and Samuels 1974). This is not to say that *only* fluent oral readers can comprehend; sometimes, readers who do not sound fluent comprehend quite well.

Ideally, fluency instruction involves supporting children in reading both smoothly and with comprehension, and literacy centers can be designed for children to work toward these goals. However, beginning readers, with their word-by-word intonation and finger pointing, often do not demonstrate fluency, and we don't expect them to until they learn to integrate decoding and comprehension processes.

Two kinds of classroom experiences have been found effective in fostering fluency for primary-grade readers: (1) repeated reading and (2) reading aloud after a teacher has modeled reading while students followed the print (Klenk and Kibby 2000; Rasinski 2004). As children work in centers, activities such as readers theatre, oral reading of poetry, shared reading of big books, paired reading, and tape-assisted reading can be used to promote reading fluency.

Tip for Differentiation

Texts used for fluency instruction should be relatively easy for the reader, or at least easy enough for successful meaning making after a teacher or peer has modeled reading the text. Looking at a book's level is not enough when considering what might be appropriate, because a child's familiarity with the book and with its content and vocabulary plays a part in how readable the text will be.

Goal 6: Expanded Uses of and Knowledge About Writing

Another goal for centers is that they will support children in expanding their uses of and knowledge about writing. Figure 2–7 offers a set of key writing competencies that centers can be designed to support.

Writing Competencies

_____ Uses writing to serve multiple functions; writes about a range of topics; chooses own topics.

_____ Uses varied resources to locate information (other children, reference books, pictionaries, the Internet).

_____ Develops rich content in writing

_____ Invents spellings, using progressively more sophisticated phonics knowledge; conventionally spells an increasing number of commonly used words.

_____ Uses punctuation and capitalization.

_____ Proofreads, revises, and edits as appropriate.

_____ Uses different voices; uses vocabulary, grammatical forms, and genres that are appropriate to goals.

Figure 2–7 *Writing Competencies*

To foster development of the competencies listed in Figure 2–7, center activities must provide opportunities for children to write for a variety of meaningful purposes. Even beginning kindergartners can do this; they can write (or pretend to write) lists, stories, notes, observations, questions, labels, and more!

Research in early childhood classrooms shows that children's writing develops in significant ways when they

- have ample time to write

- experiment with varied genres and content

- have access to literacy materials in their play

- control writing decisions

- are free to use classroom resources to support their writing

- write and share their writing in a social community

- use writing as a tool to achieve authentic learning and communicating goals (Dyson 1989; Edelsky 1986; Goodman and Wilde 1992; Graves 1983)

As you plan and observe your writing centers, use elements such as these to evaluate the quality of your students' experiences.

Tip for Differentiation

For each child, motivation to write comes from topics that are of interest and personal relevance. Therefore, try to avoid giving lots of writing prompts. Prompts do not serve the purpose of differentiating. Some teachers make the mistake of assuming that some children have nothing to write about. Any child who has a sibling or a pet; a favorite television show or a favorite athlete; something she or he loves or something she or he detests has something to write about! Provide young learners with support in identifying *their* topics. Begin by choosing three topics that *you* would like to write about and discussing them with your students.

Goal 7: Vocabulary

Finally, centers are a place for children to develop their vocabularies. An important idea for teachers—probably *the* most important idea for vocabulary instruction—is that words are learned *as concepts, not just as words*. "In order to know a word we must have at least as strong an understanding of the context as we do the definition" (Brozo 2003, 47). For example, to understand the word *float*, a child needs to have a feel for the many contexts in which the word takes on meaning. This feel comes from playing around with floating and sinking objects, discussing the properties of these objects and the relationships between them, and using the word in various contexts across various situations. It also helps to *read*, because reading provides yet another context for understanding a word's meanings.

It is rather obvious that vocabulary is important for talking, and for writing, but it is also important for reading. Learning new concepts and the words that are associated with them is essential for comprehension *and* decoding development (National Research Council 1998). This is to say that the more developed a child's vocabulary, the easier it is for that child to *understand* vocabulary-rich text and the easier it becomes to *decode* it. Think about which of the following is easier for you to *decode* and *understand*:

■ "That's a gutta-percha point," replied the doc (Brown 2003, 88).

   ___ Easy to decode?   ___ Easy to understand?

■ The Csikszentmihalyis further contend that we can get into the "magical state" of flow every day (Jensen 2000, 130).

   ___ Easy to decode?   ___ Easy to understand?

Your level of understanding, and your ability to read without extensive effort at decoding, will depend on which of the concepts and related vocabulary you have heard and experienced. Familiar concepts and familiar vocabulary make decoding and understanding easier.

A wide body of research on vocabulary development suggests that words are best learned when students

- experience a word-rich environment in which attention is given to interesting and new words;

- are repeatedly exposed to words in a variety of contexts;

- are active in exploring word meanings and learning strategies to figure out word meanings; and

- make personal connections to word meanings (Blachowicz and Fisher 2000).

Developmentally appropriate literacy centers should be designed for children to experience and explore words in these ways.

Tip for Differentiation

When working with bilingual or English language learners, keep in mind the importance of *context* in learning new words. When you are working with English text, to help clarify the context, read very expressively, use gestures and facial expressions, help children make connections between words and illustrations, and use props to illustrate words and events. Also, provide bilingual books (books with the full text in both languages) and text pairs (one book in each language).

CHAPTER 3

Organizing the Physical Environment for Centers

Aisha appears purposeful and relaxed as she begins her center work one morning in her well-organized classroom environment. For the hour, her center team has four center choices. The choices are strategically located close together to avoid lots of crisscrossing traffic with other teams.

Aisha begins her work in the classroom library, where a set of books focusing on birds is neatly arranged on a shelf. The arrangement is appealing: six of the books are displayed upright, and the rest are stacked in three bins, one for nonfiction, one for fiction, and one for poetry. After choosing a book of poems, Aisha kicks off her boots, settles on a comfortable cushion, and begins to read silently. But before long, she is poking at Javier with her toes and laughing wildly at his resulting wiggles and grimaces. When their teacher, Ron, hears the children's laughter, he leans away from his small reading group to check on the noise. After all, these children are working near him in the designated "hush zone" of the classroom. He smiles—but points suggestively at the children who are trying to read with him—and it works. Aisha and Javier know what to do in the hush zone, and they know that they may move to another area if they feel like talking and laughing. They get back to their reading, and Ron moves on with his group.

After reading for a while, Aisha moves to her next center. Here, materials for "reading the room" are stored. Aisha picks up a clipboard, a pad of sticky notes, and a pencil. She rereads an instruction card that Ron has already read to the class and then sets off, looking for words that begin or end with *ch* or *sh*. Later, the class will use these words to write poetry that alliterates. After recording eight words, Aisha places her work in a centrally located manila folder that is labeled with her name and replaces the clipboard and the pencil to their designated storage area. Just as she begins to check the center schedule board to see where she can go next, her teacher calls her to participate in a small reading group.

Because Aisha is often easily distracted, and because her interactions with other children could sometimes be characterized as aggressive, she does especially well in a physical environment that is carefully and sensitively organized. The physical environment in her classroom helps her stay on track. It is appealing to children; it allows for choice, movement, talk, and laughter; and it provides information about what to do in various centers, how much noise is acceptable, and which centers are "hers" for the day. Aisha is just one child, but Ron has twenty-seven students this year. He counts on the physical environment to help him do his teaching and managing.

The physical environment in a classroom greatly influences children's learning, actions, and behaviors. The design of the environment can lead to noise, tension, frustration, and confusion (where, especially for some children, not much literacy learning occurs) or to orderliness, appropriate challenges, and peacefulness (where all children's literacy has a chance to develop). This chapter contains tips and ideas for arranging and differentiating the physical environment of your classroom so that it supports productive center-based activity.

Creating Space for Centers

As you are preparing for center-based instruction, first think about how many centers you would like to regularly offer. Teachers typically offer anywhere from four to twelve centers on a given day. When you have decided on the number, list or sketch out all of the places in the classroom that the centers might be located. Careful placement is especially important in small classrooms, where creative use of every nook and cranny becomes essential. Center space may be created using

- student tables or clusters of desks
- mats or thick rugs
- the area of the classroom that is used for whole-group instruction
- a shelf or a counter along the wall
- pocket charts
- tubs or envelopes of materials that children can take anywhere in the classroom

- a wheeled cart

- the computer area

- the class library

- the sociodramatic play area

- wall space (to hang necessary materials)

In small classrooms, student tables or clusters of desks often become centers just during center time. Materials that are stored in bins or envelopes are used at these tables during center time, as well as in other parts of the classroom, and are then put away again when center time is over. With creative planning, even in a small classroom, center-based instruction is possible. Figure 3–1 shows a small classroom that is arranged for twenty-five to thirty children to work in twelve centers (eleven for center work and one for small-group instruction with the teacher).

Laying Out the Centers

Finding space for your centers is a start, but the subsequent planning and placing that you do will be the essence of what makes your environment successful. Ideally, you should create your center space through a carefully planned, child-sensitive arrangement of furniture and materials. The following guidelines may be helpful as you consider the layout of your centers.

Fixed Areas

Arrange centers that must be placed in fixed areas first. Fixed areas are those that make use of materials or furniture that is not easy to rearrange. For example, arrange the listening center, computer center, and transparency machine first because they will need to be placed near electrical outlets. Arrange art and science activities near trash cans and sinks; arrange the big-book center at the easel; arrange the writing center near the pencil sharpener; avoid having outside light reflect off the computer screen; and so on.

Boundaries

Use shelves, tables, and other furniture to *establish clear boundaries between center areas.* Large, open spaces entice some children to run, chase one another, and engage in large motor play. Smaller, confined spaces invite constructive activity and quieter, thoughtful talk (Johnson, Christie, and Yawkey 1987; Roskos 1995). Establishing boundaries should not mean that materials may not be carried back and forth. In fact, allowing children to retrieve materials of their choosing and carry them across center boundaries extends their creativity and thinking and helps ensure that their individual interests and strengths are being capitalized on.

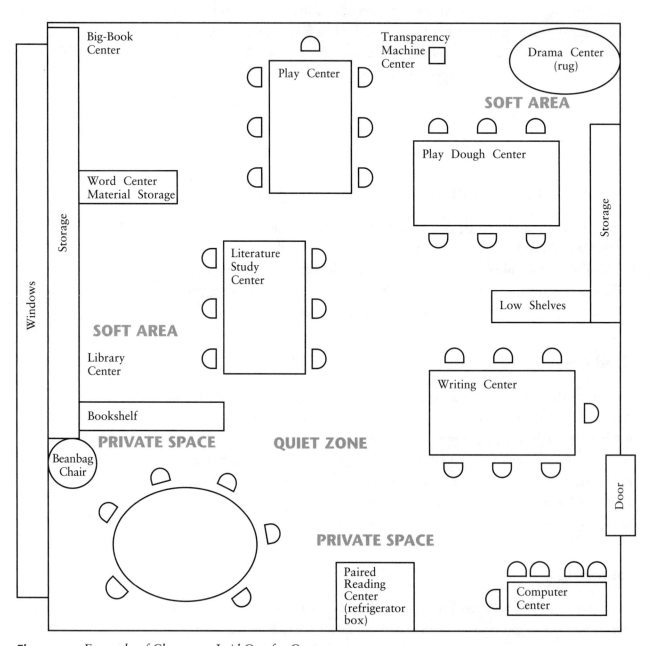

Figure 3–1 *Example of Classroom Laid Out for Centers*

Tip for Differentiation

Whenever possible, ask students for ideas regarding materials to include in the centers. For example, in one classroom, a child requested that the CD player be placed in the drama center so that the children could find music to accompany their dramatic retellings. Another requested that a basket of squishy toys be placed in the reading center "to help [students] read better and act good." Yet another requested that students be permitted to bring small toys into the writing center, "because that's what [they] like to write about most, and toys could help [them]."

Traffic

Purposefully plan traffic patterns. First, direct traffic away from areas that require privacy or intense concentration. Also, avoid heavy traffic through areas with electrical cords or open containers of liquid, or where block structures may be knocked down or painters' elbows bumped.

Second, as an overall goal, plan for *minimal* traffic. If groups of children have more than one center to choose from, keep each group's choices as close together as possible. For example, if one group of children may rotate among three choices, try to keep those three centers together in terms of physical space. If some groups will not be rotating during center time, take advantage of the lack of traffic that will result from these areas. Figure 3–2 illustrates a desirable traffic pattern and an undesirable one. The desirable pattern shows

Desirable Traffic Pattern

Undesirable Traffic Pattern

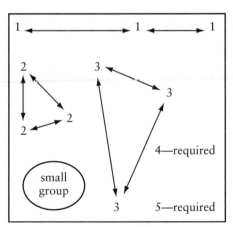
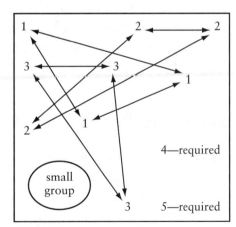

Figure 3–2 *Desirable and Undesirable Traffic Patterns*

how five groups of children could be organized for minimal traffic. (Groups 1, 2, and 3 rotate among three choices for the period; groups 4 and 5 do not rotate.) The undesirable pattern shows lots of crisscrossing and confusion.

Small-Group Teaching Area

Select a quiet corner for small-group instruction. If you plan to regularly work with small groups as most students are working in centers, it is important to give high priority to setting up a suitable space for this work. The area should be relatively private and quiet, and it should have very good lighting, preferably natural lighting. If you want to use a tape recorder, be sure you'll have access to an electrical outlet. Regardless of whether you have another adult in the classroom when you are working with small groups, you will want to sit facing the classroom so that you can help monitor activities. And it makes sense that you would want the children who are working with you to have their heads turned away from the bulk of the activity.

Quiet Zone

Establish a quiet zone. To create a quiet zone, place all of the quiet centers in the same part of the classroom (Brewer 1992). Quiet zones provide an atmosphere for the kind of concentration and collaboration that are needed for activities such as small-group instruction, independent reading, partner reading, and collaborative writing. Noisier centers, such as a drama center and a center for choral reading, should be concentrated in another part of the classroom.

Tip for Differentiation

Use the quiet zone as an area where individuals or groups may go to work on an impromptu basis, as it best suits their needs. Some children regularly work better in a quieter space.

Selecting Props and Materials

Considering general props and materials is another important component of designing the overall center space. Props and materials can do much to contribute to a well-managed, comfortable, and inviting learning environment for all. The following guidelines may be helpful as you consider the general design of your centers.

Choice

To the extent that it is possible, *provide children with choices of what to read and write, choices of activities, and choices of ways to demonstrate their understandings*. Choice allows children to do their own differentiating, which helps ensure that they are working in areas of interest and with materials and activities that are appropriately challenging.

Tip for Differentiation

Meet individually with students who do not regularly make learning choices that allow for them to be successful. For example, if you have students who regularly choose reading material that is too difficult, pull them aside. Discuss which books would better suit their needs and, if necessary, *assign* those books rather than allow for completely open choices. If you have a child who can express more through drawing than writing, encourage that mode of expression for some center activities.

Collaborative Activity

Arrange center materials so that they support collaborative activity. The ways in which you set up the environment for collaboration, and the types of props that you include, will influence the amount of social interactions that occur and the amount of time that children spend working and playing *together* (Petrakos and Howe 1996). Collaboration and talk are ultimate goals for center time because of their centrality to human learning. To inspire collaboration, purposefully design centers for *group activity* versus solitary activity and for *several* versus few possible uses of materials. For example, a pretend spacecraft with only *one* seat and *only* books about planets would likely yield a different and less collaborative kind of play than a spacecraft with several seats and a range of literacy materials (such as fix-it manuals, newspaper articles, books about astronauts, and empty logs for writing).

Private Spaces

Establish private spaces. Private spaces provide a relaxing retreat and allow children, if they desire, to view others without necessarily interacting with them (Lowman and Ruhmann 1998). Crowded conditions, continuous interaction, and frequent interruptions can cause fatigue and frustration for some children (Kostelnik et al. 1993) and can inadvertently lead to unnecessary conflicts. And some children simply work better on the sidelines of activity. To create private spaces, set up any of the following:

■ a children's pool stocked with pillows and cushions

■ a refrigerator box with an arched doorway, stocked with pillows

■ a loft with a private upper room

■ a table with pillows and cushions under it

■ a couch walled off by bookshelves

■ a rug in the corner, walled off by bookshelves

Tip for Differentiation

As you work toward an environment that differentiates, ensure that children who need a private retreat can find one and use it at will. Sometimes you may wish to assign a child to work in this area. With safety in mind, be sure that the private space is constructed in such a way that you are able to monitor the activity of the children using it. Do not allow a stigma to attach itself to children who work better independently (for whatever reasons, whether they be behavioral or academic). Openly discuss with all of your students the fact that different students work better in different kinds of situations.

Soft Areas

Create soft areas. Soft areas are made with pillows, cushions, colors, and curves (Brewer 1992) or with malleable play materials such as play dough, sand, and water (Kostelnik et al. 1993). Soft areas are comfortable and relaxing to children (Kostelnik et al. 1993) and allow for restful, creative expression. Consider making the private areas of your classroom (described earlier) into soft areas as well.

Book Area

Create an inviting book area as part of every set of centers. "Children spend more time interacting with books when the classroom has a comfortable, attractive book area" (Schickedanz 1999, 89). Therefore, show students how to display the books in an attractive configuration, such as standing on end, intermingled with puppets or props, grouped into a few appealing text sets, or with front covers arranged on a book stand. The book area should be carpeted, include pillows and cushions, and be quiet enough for children to hear each other reading and talking softly.

Tip for Differentiation

Center books should represent a variety of languages, cultures, religions, family structures, topics, and genres so that they appeal to and connect with a variety of children. The difficulty of the material should vary, too, so that each child has opportunities to sometimes read texts that are easy and sometimes read texts that are challenging. Don't worry about always having children read books that are written at their level. Children need to read all kinds of texts to develop a broad range of comprehension and decoding strategies.

As you monitor the book area throughout the year, keep in mind that a key characteristic of high-achieving classrooms is that the children in them spend lots of time reading. For this reason, spend some time watching the activity in this center to ensure that *reading*, rather than only talking and book browsing, is taking place. While talking and browsing are, of course, not detrimental to learning, increasing actual time spent *reading*—whether it be oral, silent, choral, or paired—has been found to enhance reading achievement (Allington 2001).

Sociodramatic Play Area

Develop a sociodramatic play area as part of every set of centers, even if you teach second or third grade. Because play is children's primary learning tool (Vygotsky 1978), children should have access to it *in school* throughout the primary years. While younger children often enjoy playing in an area set up as a restaurant, an office, a kitchen, or a store, many older children enjoy playing in roles such as journalists, reporters, teachers, toy industry workers, actors, directors, and producers.

> ## Tip for Differentiation
>
> Be sure that each child will be able to play in meaningful ways. As
> you and the children set up play areas, be sure to ask for *their* ideas
> about what they would like to play and what kinds of literacy
> materials you should incorporate. Rich literacy exploration is most
> likely to occur when children have access to familiar literacy
> materials that are reflective of their lives, cultures, and knowledge
> about the world (Neuman and Roskos 1992; Roskos 1995).

Safety

As you design centers and select materials for them, *make safety an overarching
concern*. Anticipate and prevent situations in which any type of accident (such
as tripping over a cord, slipping in water, or spilling a large amount of paint) may
occur. Keep in mind that as children move through the kindergarten and primary years, the nature of the supervision that they require changes. For example,
children learn *over time* to carry a tub of water, hammer a nail, pour paint into
a cup, or use needles and sharp scissors, and different children in your classroom
will be differently experienced with each of these. Your task during the time that
they are with you is to watch children closely, allowing their responsibility to in-
crease while always attending to what is age-appropriate and individually appropriate (Bredekamp and Copple 1997).

Considering Children's Ability to Work
in the Environment

Many young children are yet unable to identify the kinds of conditions that
help them think and work most productively. Considering the following issues
as you plan for centers may be helpful along these lines and will likely prevent
you from having to spend time working on them when centers are under way.

Movement

As you evaluate your set of centers as a whole, *reflect on the extent to which
each group of children will have opportunities to move around*. Some children
need to move more than others and find it very difficult to work if they do not
have opportunities to do so. If you have forty-five or sixty minutes planned for
centers, and any group of children will be expected to sit still the entire time,

or sit in hard chairs through all of their rotations, then learning time will likely become inefficient for some of these children. For example, if Aisha's group is expected to move from the *computer center* to the *writing center* to the *literature study center* (all relatively quiet and "hard" areas), this is likely to build more tension and fatigue than is necessary. Ensuring that at least one of the centers allows her group to use play dough, or actively play with soft puppets, or walk around the room, will likely result in less tension and fatigue and will help the children work altogether more productively.

Clutter

Avoid clutter and oversupplies of materials. If you provide too many materials at once (such as sticky notes, stickers, and blank notepads), students may use them up rather than use them constructively (Roskos 1995), and some children may become distracted or overwhelmed by the number of choices. When students are not using materials productively or appropriately, or when they are having difficulty picking up the materials and organizing them after use, the center may be overloaded.

Neatness

Ensure that areas are kept neat. Toward the end of each center period, let children know that it is time to clean up. Between each rotation, select a helper to go quickly through the room and check to see that materials in each center have been put away. The helper can quickly straighten the area if necessary, or he can ask the person who left the materials askew to return to the center and help that person in a positive way to see that the area might not be neat enough for the next group to work. The two can work together to quickly straighten the area.

Tip for Differentiation

Children have different views of the meaning of *neat* and have different experiences with picking up after themselves. For students who consistently do not leave the area ready for the next child or group, take the time to meet, to model how to clean up at school, and to clarify what a *neat* center area looks like. A few of these meetings will ultimately take less of your time (and cause less frustration for all involved) than monitoring cleanup problems day after day.

Finished and Unfinished Work

Decide on a place for children to organize the work that they produce in centers. Biederman (1999) conducted a study to investigate management issues surrounding centers. She found that without a plan, her students often did not know what to do with the work they produced. Some students left their work in centers, others lost theirs, and other work was unintentionally thrown away. Her class decided that unfinished work would be placed at students' tables for safekeeping, and each student's finished work would be kept in a center work folder. This plan allowed Biederman to track the students' work through the centers and the progress they were making throughout the week.

Tip for Differentiation

For students who need encouragement or support to give center work their best effort, ask them to give their folder directly to you at the end of center time each day. This will serve as a reminder for you to quickly check the material and to identify with the child areas that may need support or extra effort the next day.

Numbers and Materials

Decide how many children could work in each center productively and comfortably. If your students rotate from center to center in groups, be sure that large groups have enough materials to work with. If centers are open for all children's choosing, decide with your students how many children could productively work in each area, and place a number label at the center to serve as a reminder for you and the children.

Tip for Differentiation

Consider whether you have certain students who would work better in smaller groups. If most of your groups contain five or six students, would one or two groups with just two or three students in them better serve some children's needs?

Center Schedule Board

Place a schedule board for centers in clear view of most centers. Teach your students how to read the board. Because some will take longer to learn to use the board than others, encourage them to request another student's help if they are unsure of what to do.

Tip for Differentiation

After teaching the class how to use the schedule board, if necessary, pull together a small group for a minilesson focused on learning to read the board.

Figure 3–3 shows an example of a schedule board. With this particular example, after each center period, the teacher rotates the children's names. Rotations occur until all of the children have had the chance to complete each row. (See Chapter 4 for additional schedule board ideas.) Make sure you place the board in a location that will not create undue or new traffic.

Instruction Cards

In some cases, it may be worth your effort to *create instruction cards that help students remember what to do in particular centers.* Read and discuss the instructions with students before placing the card in the center for reference at a later time. You may find that only one or two students need the cards, but each time a student can do something independently, your valuable teaching time increases. Figure 3–4 provides an example instruction card.

Evaluating the Center Environment

As you can see, there is much to consider when laying out the physical space and the materials for centers. The influence that the physical design has on learning is substantial. Plan and work with your design as if the environment itself is another *teacher* in the classroom. It's that important!

When centers do not engage even one or two children, or when they do not run smoothly, it may be helpful to take a critical tour to evaluate the setup and the materials, because the barrier may lie in the physical environment. Figure 3–5 provides a form that may be used to plan and evaluate your center environment.

	Center Schedule		
Names	*Choices for the Day*		
1. 2. 3. 4. 5.	Big Books	Transparency Machine	Drama
1. 2. 3. 4. 5.	Words	Class Library	Literature Study
1. 2. 3. 4. 5.	Play	Partner Read	Play Dough
1. 2. 3. 4. 5.	Writing		
1. 2. 3. 4. 5.	Computers		

Figure 3–3 *Center Schedule Board*

Instruction Card for Word Center

1. Place two sticky notes on clipboard.
2. Label one CH and one SH.
3. Walk around room to find words that *begin* or *end* with CH or SH.
4. Record *eight* words total.

Figure 3–4 *Instruction Card for Word Center*

Figure 3–5 *Form for Evaluating Your Center Environment*

Evaluation of Center Environment

Rate each item on the chart: 1—Excellent 2—Good 3—Fair 4—Needs Improvement												
List a brief title for each center in the space provided at right.	1	2	3	4	5	6	7	8	9	10	11	12
Center activities appeal to children.												
Center is comfortable for the intended activity.												
Materials inspire children to talk and collaborate as appropriate to the activity.												
Center allows for a level of concentration appropriate to the activity.												
Center materials and layout are safe.												
Center is in view of an adult.												
Boundaries between this and other centers are clear.												
Traffic near center is low.												
Adequate materials are available.												
Center is easy to clean up.												
Center maintains an inviting appearance after children have used it.												
Children have enough time to complete center activities.												
Activities are at an appropriate level (or adapted) for all children to participate.												
Children have choices that allow them to differentiate for themselves.												
Children know where to store finished and unfinished center work.												
Indicate which centers fall into the following categories.												
Quiet Zone—Q												
Private Space—P												
Soft Area—S												
Allows for Movement—M												

CHAPTER 4

Managing Center-Based Instruction

In many classrooms, the professional skill that goes into a well-organized center time seems to hide itself after the first month or two of school. When I visit a classroom after the middle of October or so, I often notice how smoothly the centers are running—without much help from the teacher. Usually, children are working actively and industriously. They are reading, writing, talking, listening, drawing, playing, and thinking. They look like they are having fun, and when I listen to their language, I can tell that they are learning. If it is a first-through third-grade classroom, the teacher is often working in a corner with a small reading or writing group. She spends some of her time there, but she also spends time providing and differentiating instruction as she moves from center to center. In kindergarten classrooms, the teacher spends a bit more time working with the children at the centers, but she still pulls away to work with small groups.

Curious about the construction of a well-organized center-based classroom, I have spent time talking and working with numerous exemplary teachers and observing their classrooms. I have formally studied several of these teachers' classrooms, spending anywhere from one week to eight months in them. On the following pages, we will examine the organizational techniques that these teachers—and many others—have found helpful in implementing centers. Specifically, we will look at

■ models for organizing children to rotate through centers

■ tips for getting center routines and activities to run smoothly

■ tips for working with transitions

Deciding on a Model for Rotation

A number of models are available for organizing children to rotate through centers. Deciding on the best model for you requires considering a number of variables. For example, how long will your students be working in centers each day? How many centers per day should they attend? Does it matter? Should some centers be required and some optional? Should students be placed in groups to work in centers? If so, how many times per day (if any) should the groups rotate? Or should individual students have complete freedom to move independently from center to center?

Deciding between planned rotation of groups and individual freedom to wander can be tricky. On one hand, spending only twenty or thirty minutes in a center and then being expected to rotate is going to present difficulties for some children. When working on something interesting, it is hard to just drop everything and switch focus—and if a child is focused on learning, it may not be the best practice to force an abrupt switch. On the other hand, children who work independently through completely open centers sometimes choose the same centers day after day, gaining little experience with new activities or working with different children.

This section contains some rotation models for you to consider. They vary in terms of how children are scheduled to rotate and how many activities children have to choose from per session. Selecting the best model for you and your students will likely take some mixing, experimentation, and adaptation, and you will probably continue to adapt year after year as *you* change and as you work with different groups of children. As you design your own model, keep in mind that two to six children could work together in a center at any given time. If you want your students to work in groups of two, then two or three pairs could work together at a center at the same time.

Who Works Together?

A review of research and theory suggests that centers work to their best advantage when children with varying capabilities work together in them (Kopacz 2003; Slavin 1987). If during centers you decide to work with small reading groups, and if these groups have been formed based on the difficulty of text the children are reading, then these groups should *not* move through centers together. Heterogeneous (mixed-ability) groups lead to higher-quality experiences for all children. "Heterogeneity creates variability and differences that lead to intellectual tension and socio-cognitive conflict. This conflict or tension is resolved through verbal interaction, which in turn leads to the development of thinking" (Ben-Ari 2004, 9).

Tip for Differentiation

Plan for center activities to include *varied topics* and *varied ways to demonstrate knowledge* so that different children—all children—can step forward at different times to take on the responsibility of initiating discussions, explaining, modeling, and problem solving. Trust that children's *different* kinds of knowledge and *different* ways of knowing will prompt them into meaningful collaboration and new ways of thinking.

What Does the Teacher Do?

You have some choices regarding your own activity during center time. You may wish to keep your time completely open to oversee centers and to work with individual students. If you choose this role, you may find that less structure is needed in terms of the rotation model you select and the activities you assign.

If you meet with small groups of readers or writers during center time, then building in more structure (especially at first) will help center workers to proceed independently. If you plan for a ninety-minute center time, depending on the grade you teach, you could probably work with three or four small groups each day. One option is to have children in centers rotate every thirty minutes and to call groups to come and work with you at the beginning of each rotation; another is to simply call children away from activities as you are ready to work with them.

Tip for Differentiation

Consider spending the first thirty minutes of center time providing individualized support for students working in centers. Then move to small-group instruction.

What Do the Rotation Models Look Like?

Three models for children to rotate through centers are common in early childhood classrooms:

■ *Individual Pace:* All centers are open for students to self-select activities for the day.

■ *Group-in-One-Center:* Each child is assigned to a group that attends one center together during the center period. Group members stay together.

■ *Group with Choice:* Each child is assigned to a group whose individuals may choose from more than one center. Group members may split up.

Whatever type of model they choose, teachers typically arrange for ten to fifteen minutes of whole-class sharing after centers are complete. Ideas for implementing each model follow.

Individual pace model

In an *individual pace model*, rather than rotate through centers as part of a group, individual students self-select centers, rotating from one to the next as they choose to do so. To help children work in this type of model, teachers list center choices on the chalkboard or a piece of chart paper, as in Figures 4–1 and 4–2. To support younger children, or children who are unable to read the chart, teachers often use pictures or icons to facilitate independent reading of the choices.

A brief planning period before center time begins helps children think about their personal preferences and supports their knowing what to do without your guidance. Children may use the planning period to talk about their choices or to record them in writing.

Tip for Differentiation

Use the planning period to set daily goals with children who have difficulty managing their time or self-regulating their behaviors during center time. (A goal sheet appears later in this chapter in Figure 4–12.) Or use this time to touch base about any academic accommodations you have made for particular students. For example, you might let a group of children know that during the last twenty minutes, you will be providing a minilesson for them. Or you could let individuals know about accommodations you have prepared such as having an adult volunteer take dictation for an activity, using a simplified graphic organizer, or choosing a book from a particular bin rather than from all of the choices at the center.

Center Choices

1. Classroom Library
2. Big Books
3. Drama
4. Listening
5. Play
6. Word Play
7. Writing
8. Content Reading Activity

Figure 4–1 *Center Choices: Brief List*

Center Choices

1. *Classroom Library*	Read any book and draw a picture about it.
2. *Big Books*	Mrs. B. (kindergarten teacher) needs us! She needs a set of puppets for each big book at this center. Choose one book and work with a partner to make a set of characters.
3. *Drama*	Choose one of the scripts and read it aloud with others.
4. *Listening*	Make a tape for one of the books. Practice reading it aloud before taping.
5. *Play*	Use the blocks, miniature animals, note cards, and markers in any way you wish.
6. *Word Play*	Use one of the blank forms to make a word search.
7. *Writing*	Write a story and make it into a book. *or* Write about something you know lots about and make a book.
8. *Content Reading Activity*	Read one of the books and use a blank transparency sheet to write down three new things you have learned. Share with the class after center time.

Figure 4–2 *Center Choices: Detailed Description*

Figures 4–3 and 4–4 provide examples of forms that children may use to create written plans. If center periods begin with all children writing plans, you can see one by one that each child gets a good start on the first activity. On both of the planning forms, children may record what they would like to do for the day, place a check next to the centers they actually attend, and afterward, write or draw about something that they learned.

Tip for Differentiation

Arrange a small-group minilesson for children who need additional discussion about or modeling of how to create and carry out a plan.

If you prefer to have a little more influence over what children do in an individual pace model, an alternative to an open list (as in Figure 4–1 or 4–2) is to designate some centers as must-do activities. On the chart that children refer to, list the set of must-do requirements along with a set of may-do choices (as in Figure 4–5). Children could do one must-do per day for a week, and if they have time at the end of each day, they could opt for a may-do. Or they could complete must-dos during the week before completing the may-dos toward the end of the week.

Tip for Differentiation

If you have children who may not be able to complete an activity because they will be out of the room for special services, consider reducing the number of must-dos, or ask the special education teacher to complete the must-do activity with the child.

Group-in-one-center model

Instead of organizing for children to rotate individually, you may prefer to place children in groups to rotate through centers. In a *group-in-one-center model*, each child is assigned to a heterogeneous group for the day, for a whole week, or even longer. Each group is assigned to a center. The group members may do just one activity, such as writing a story or reading aloud, or each center area may offer several activities, allowing the children to choose which they

Figure 4–3 *Written or Drawn Plans for the Day*

Write or Draw Plans for the Day

Name: _____ Date: _____

My plans:

Something I learned today:

Figure 4–4 *Written Plans for the Week*

Write Plans for the Week

Name: _____

Monday Plans	Tuesday Plans	Wednesday Plans	Thursday Plans	Friday Plans
1. _____	1. _____	1. _____	1. _____	1. _____
2. _____	2. _____	2. _____	2. _____	2. _____
3. _____	3. _____	3. _____	3. _____	3. _____
Something I learned today:	Something I learned today:	Something I learned today:	Something I learned today:	Something I learned today:

Center Choices

Must Do

1. *Partner Corner:*
   Read your Friday take-home book to a partner. Listen to a partner read.

2. *Writing Center:*
   Draw and illustrate one thing you have learned so far about ants.

3. *Word Play:*
   Use letter tiles to plan a word search using ten words from the word wall. Write the letters on a word search sheet. Trade with a friend.

4. *Class Library:*
   Choose any book you like from the top shelf and read it.

5. *Observation:*
   Observe the ant farm and write down at least one question about ants.

May Do

6. Listening Center

7. Write or draw at your table.

8. Read at your table.

9. Play Area

10. Big-Book Center

Figure 4–5 *Must-Do and May-Do Center Choices*

would like to do within the center that day (or week). For example, a *reading center* might offer all of the following:

- big books (varied levels and topics) to be read with pointers

- a pocket chart for sentence-strip sequencing and reading

- small books (varied levels and topics) for partners to read together

- materials with which to write and draw a retelling of a book the class has read and discussed

- a set of puppets or felt pieces with which to retell a familiar story

In a forty-five- to sixty-minute period, students might accomplish anywhere from one to five activities within the center. Figure 4–6 provides an example of a teacher plan for a group-in-one-center model, and Figure 4–7 provides a blank form that may be used for your planning.

Group with choice models

In a *group with choice model*, students are assigned to a group whose individual members may choose from *more than one center*. Unlike the group-in-one-center model, children may split up and work in different centers depending on the activities they choose. Figures 4–8, 4–9, 4–10, and 4–11 show some possibilities and examples for organizing a group with choice model.

Getting Routines and Activities to Run Smoothly

In order for students to work confidently and independently in centers, they need a clear sense of the routines that will be followed in your classroom and a clear sense of your expectations for specific activities. Making time in the early days to establish clear routines and expectations will free you up later to work with small groups or with individual students.

Establish Clear Routines and Expectations

Do the following on the first days of centers:

- Show children how to use the schedule board to get to the appropriate center.

- As students work, begin to help them know what is expected in terms of quality of work. Don't wait until the end of the center period or the end of the day to have discussions about quality. Support children *as they are working* so that they don't become frustrated or lose their momentum.

- Model how to tidy up centers and prepare them for the next group.

- Walk students through any rotations that are required.

Group-in-One-Center Model

Names	Center	Choices for the Day
1. 2. 3. 4. 5.	Reading	• Read poetry from the books at the center. • Choose a poem and practice reading it aloud to a friend. If you wish, share it with the class. • Read a poem into the tape recorder. Listen and then read again, trying to improve how you sound.
1. 2. 3. 4. 5.	Writing	• Write a poem in free verse. • Write an acrostic poem. • Copy a poem that you like.
1. 2. 3. 4. 5.	Vocabulary and Words	• Choose a color. Work collaboratively to think of all the words you can to describe that color. • Choose a state. Work collaboratively to think of all the words you can to describe that state. • Browse through one of the textbooks on this table and find two words whose meaning you do not know. Find the meanings and be ready to tell the class how and where you found them.
1. 2. 3. 4. 5.	Social Studies	• Draw a map of the route you take to school. • Use the U.S. map to choose a state that you would like to visit. Write down one reason that you would like to visit that state. Look up that state in one of the reference books and add two more reasons. • Draw a map of our school. • Make a list of the places in our classroom where you can find a map.
1. 2. 3. 4. 5.	Play	• Use the play dough to construct a model of a perfect classroom. • Use the play dough to construct a model of a perfect bedroom. • Draw a map of a perfect classroom. • Draw a map of a perfect bedroom.

Figure 4–6 *Group-in-One-Center Model Example*

Figure 4–7 *Group-in-One-Center Model Planning Form*

Group-in-One-Center Model

Names	Center	Choices for the Day
1. 2. 3. 4. 5.		
1. 2. 3. 4. 5.		
1. 2. 3. 4. 5.		
1. 2. 3. 4. 5.		
1. 2. 3. 4. 5.		

Group-in-One-Center Model
Number of sessions: One per day (45–60 minutes)
Activity choices per session: One to five
Number of sessions to complete a full rotation: Five
Using the board: Rotate names at the beginning of each day. Groups do not rotate during the center period.

Figure 4–8 *Group with Choice Model 1 Planning Form*

Group with Choice Model 1

Names	Choices for 30 Minutes (or 45 Minutes)	
1. 2. 3. 4. 5.		
1. 2. 3. 4. 5.		
1. 2. 3. 4. 5.		
1. 2. 3. 4. 5.		
1. 2. 3. 4. 5.		
1. 2. 3. 4. 5.		

Group with Choice Model 1
Number of sessions: One or two per day
Activity choices per session: Two
Number of sessions to complete a full rotation: Six
Using the board: Rotate names after 30 or 45 minutes.

Group with Choice Model 1

Names	Choices for 30 Minutes (or 45 Minutes)	
1. 2. 3. 4. 5.	Big Books at Easel	Paired Reading
1. 2. 3. 4. 5.	Drama Center	Storytelling Center
1. 2. 3. 4. 5.	Science Observation	Science Reading
1. 2. 3. 4. 5.	Play Dough	Home Living Area
1. 2. 3. 4. 5.	Word Center	Book Writing
1. 2. 3. 4. 5.	Independent Reading	Clipboard Activity

Figure 4–9 *Group with Choice Model 1 Example*

Figure 4–10 *Group with Choice Model 2 Planning Form*

Group with Choice Model 2

Names	Choices for Two Days		
1. 2. 3. 4. 5. 6. 7.			
1. 2. 3. 4. 5. 6. 7.			
1. 2. 3. 4. 5. 6. 7.			
1. 2. 3. 4. 5. 6. 7.			

Group with Choice Model 2
Number of sessions: One per day or one session that lasts for two days
Activity choices per session: Three
Number of sessions to complete a full rotation: Four
Using the board: Rotate names after one day or two days.

Figure 4–11 *Group with Choice Model 3 Planning Form*

Group with Choice Model 3

Names	Choices for One Day		
1. 2. 3. 4. 5.	Center 1	Center 2	Center 3
1. 2. 3. 4. 5.	Center 4	Center 5	Center 6
1. 2. 3. 4. 5.	Center 7		Center 8
1. 2. 3. 4. 5.	Center 9 REQUIRED		
1. 2. 3. 4. 5.	Center 10 REQUIRED		

Group with Choice Model 3
Number of sessions: One or two per day
Activity choices per session: One to three
Number of sessions to complete a full rotation: Five
Using the board: Rotate names after 3–60 minutes.

■ Discuss how and when to take restroom breaks.

■ Let students know how to request your attention when you are working with a small group.

Even with these elements in place, as you begin to pull away to work with small groups during center time, you will likely experience many interruptions. Interruptions are to be *expected*, but right from the start, encourage children to collaborate with and seek help from one another rather than depend on you for support. Make it clear right away that the children are not to call loudly for you or to interrupt your group. Suggest a low-key signal that they may use to capture your attention when necessary, such as writing their name on a sticky note and handing it to you or approaching your table with one finger raised. Encourage children to go back and do what they can until you can come and assist rather than wait by your table until you can break. This will begin to foster their independence.

Tip for Differentiation

Take note of children who seem unable (for whatever reasons) to proceed without your support. Don't give up on children who don't fall into the routine after the first few weeks, and don't assume that this is just the way things have to be. These children often just need some extra support or accommodations (see Chapter 5) to make centers work for them. Consider working with the children through the goal sheet featured later in this chapter (Figure 4–12).

Observe

For the first weeks, try to allow yourself to spend much of center time closely monitoring your students' center activity. This will help you decide on the kinds of literacy activities that will be appropriate for centers, and it is a good time to take note of the kinds of things that students request your help with, for example, "no eraser," "not sharing," "hungry," "forgot to tell me—leaving at noon," "doesn't know what to do," "activity too difficult." Try to categorize these notes in a way that helps you sort out the source of most needs and determine which students will need extra support. When center time is not running smoothly or when individual children are having difficulty, any range of sensations—from hurt feelings to hunger to boredom to frustration—may make it difficult for them to concentrate and learn. Look for the source of each problem and tackle it head on.

After the first few days of centers, you may wish to draw the class together to discuss or role-play scenarios such as

- what to do if a student isn't sure about which center to go to next

- what to do if a student isn't sure how to do an activity

- what to do if a student doesn't have enough materials

- what to do if another child is preventing a student from participating effectively in center activities

You may also wish to arrange whole-class meetings to discuss what is going well and not well with centers. Record students' ideas and follow up as necessary.

For individual students, you will need to identify the specific areas that will require differentiated support. You may find it helpful to categorize your observations into three categories:

- instruction (for example, needs support reading the center materials)

- materials and activities (for example, needs materials with same content but simpler text)

- logistics (for example, needs a longer time frame to complete an activity)

Chapter 5 contains ideas for differentiating instruction in each of these areas.

As you get your students going with centers, maintain your high expectations. Expect that center time will go smoothly and expect that centers will support active learning for *all* children. Pursue these goals until you achieve them. Even teachers in classrooms with many children categorized as having learning-related difficulties or emotional disturbances are finding that during center time, these difficulties and problems seem to temporarily retreat. There's something special about centers that makes high-quality learning possible for all.

Model and Discuss Activities

Modeling particular activities before implementing them is another way to help foster confidence and independence. Although the specific ways of participating in center activities should emerge from the children's interests and understandings, for some experiences, it is helpful to model for children the basics of what you expect them to do. For example, if you want them to construct a word search or use a graphic organizer, then working through the whole process with the whole class may help them to work independently later on.

If activities are such that the whole class can practice them first, you may want to take a run through them during a whole-group work time. For example, if you would like for children to use a graphic organizer to retell a story, modeling the procedures for the class and perhaps giving the children an opportunity to experiment with the organizers will help them work independently later on. As you plan for centers, make it a regular practice to consider what might be appropriately modeled before children work at the centers independently.

> ## Tip for Differentiation
>
> Always consider whether your modeling and instruction would be more appropriate for a small group or the whole class. Sometimes it is just a small group who needs that bit of extra support.

Set Individual Conduct Goals with Students as Needed

In addition to differentiating academic support, you may wish to set individual conduct goals with students who need help engaging in appropriate actions or behaviors during center time. In most classrooms, these plans are constructed jointly between teachers and select students. Figure 4–12 provides a form that can be used for such planning.

As a rule of thumb when developing such a plan, choose positive wording that indicates what *to* do rather than what *not* to do. For example, "Clean up materials before moving on to another center" works better than "Don't leave materials out"; "Use thoughtful words" works better than "Don't call names or fight." Really, it is *normal* for children to differ in the ways they approach others and react to center activities, and all goal plans should send the message that *we're doing this together to help you learn in centers* rather than *I'm doing this to you because you aren't behaving.*

Families may be brought into the goal-planning process by discussing and jointly deciding on goals at conferences, by email, or over the phone. You can send the goal sheets home at the end of the day or week. And you can provide families with blank sheets if they wish to use a similar goal-setting format at home.

Goals

Name: _____ Date(s): _____

My goals for center time:

1.

2.

3.

How did I do?

I recommend that you avoid offering external rewards such as stickers or prizes when children accomplish their goals. Too often, when the rewards stop, so do the desired actions and behaviors. And a wide body of research shows that people who expect to be rewarded for something do not perform as well as those who do not expect to be rewarded (Kohn 1993). Let children learn to experience as a reward the sense of accomplishment and the pleasure that they achieve from successfully completing a day of worthwhile, fun, friendship-filled activities. If you want to give your students treats, do so randomly, saying, "It's just because I like you."

Figure 4–13 provides a worksheet that you may use to plan for differentiation and to set goals for children who may need extra support. Figure 5–2 (Chapter 5) shows an example of the worksheet in use.

Working with Transitions

All center models involve one type of transition or another. Some require that children switch after twenty or thirty minutes; some require that children leave everything after a designated time period and finish it the next day. Because some children are by nature slow with transitions, and because some find transitions difficult (and because both of these tendencies often lead to management difficulties), you may wish to have a plan in place to support children during transitions. Figure 4–14 offers some tips for successful transitions.

The Best Time to Learn and Teach

I believe that a well-organized, carefully crafted center time offers *the* best time to learn and teach. In terms of learning, centers allow children to work at their own paces, toward goals that are relevant to them, with accommodations and differentiation built in as they are needed. Children who have difficulty working effectively with others, or working effectively in typical school settings, can be systematically and gently supported in constructing knowledge and in learning to regulate and manage their own behaviors at school. Because you are not leading the group at the moment, you can take the time to facilitate collaboration among children and to provide all kinds of individualized support.

In terms of teaching, centers allow you the time to watch children (yes, watching is teaching; teachers who do *not* take time to watch cannot teach effectively!), to scaffold children's intellectual pursuits, and to capture their teachable moments. A well-crafted center time allows children to take the lead and set a meaningful course for their own construction of knowledge.

Figure 4–13 *Organizing for Differentiated Instruction Planning Form*

Child's Name	Centers Needing Accommodations	Other Support

© 2005 Gretchen Owocki from *Time for Literacy Centers*. Portsmouth, NH: Heinemann.

Tips for Transitions

- Make it part of your routine to go over the center schedule board before center time begins. Point out the transitions and discuss when they will take place.

- Use a timer with a visible, moving hand to help younger children keep track of the time and anticipate when transitions are about to occur.

- Give a five-minute and a one-minute notice as transitions are about to occur.

- Use a consistent cue to signal a transition (chime, flicker of lights, piano chord, familiar tune on a xylophone).

- Have a clear picture in your mind of what a transition should look like. From day one, communicate your expectations by providing explicit directions and actively orchestrating the children's transition activity.

- Gather the class for a minute or two between rotations at seats or on a carpeted area. Talk them through where they will go next and see if there are questions. (This is usually necessary only until they have learned the routine.)

- Take a snack or a bathroom break between transitions so that children have extra time to finish up their activities if they choose.

- If you work with small groups during center time, consider working with *one* group per rotation. This will minimize the number of switches that children need to make.

- Allow children who have difficulty with transitions to be responsible for helping you watch the clock or the timer and rotate the names on the schedule board when it is time to make a transition.

- If you have just a few children who do not transition easily, do not require all of the children to wait until these children are ready to move on. Make sure that most children are started on the next activity and then support the children who transition slowly or with difficulty.

- Make accommodations for students who might benefit from them. For example, allow a deeply engaged child to continue working rather than make a transition to the next center or talk a child systematically through a few transitions.

- Arrange a cleanup partner for children who make slow or difficult transitions.

Figure 4–14 *Tips for Transitions*

Differentiating the Instruction

Christian Bush has just introduced a *weather center* to her classroom. She is now observing and taking notes as the children work and play in this center. Some of the children are writing weather reports; some are reading their reports aloud; others are creating oral reports on the spot. Grace is enthusiastically (and with painstaking detail) telling some of the other children what she is going to write about.

Right now, Christian is focusing her observation on Jake. As he points to a map that he has drawn of Michigan and part of Canada, he says, "In Grand Blanc, it will be very rainy . . . but in the Upper Peninsula, it will be very sunny. In Davison, it will be cloudy and . . . in Mexico [pointing to Canada] it will be snowy." When he finishes the report, Christian points to the place that he has referred to as Mexico and then shows him on a globe the country that is *actually* north of Michigan. As she helps him notice the first three letters of the word, Jake responds, "Oh, that would be Canada!"

As Christian continues to observe, she has an "itch." Some of the children are capable of reading more than just the words and the short phrases that they have written. Although the center contains some excellent books on weather, they do not appear to suit the children's interests at the moment. "I have an idea," she tells a couple of the children and then gestures for them to follow her. She goes over to the computer, where she locates some current weather reports online.

Mark comes away from the computer reading a report from Maine. "This is the important stuff," he informs one of the other reporters. "Maine has to know it. There's going to be a flood in Maine and people have to know that."

Grace is still telling children about what she plans to write, but she has not yet written a word.

What Does Differentiated Instruction Look Like?

In this example from Christian's first-grade classroom, do you see the differentiation happening? Do you see any possibilities for differentiation that, as the teacher, you might implement during the rest of the center period or even over the next week? I will use Christian's example to begin our discussion of how teachers can use center time to differentiate their literacy instruction. To differentiate an experience for a child or group of children, a teacher may vary any of the following three elements, either *on the spot* or through *structured planning*:

1. the instructional support

2. the materials and activities

3. the logistics

Figure 5–1 synthesizes some of the typical methods that early childhood teachers use to differentiate their center-based literacy instruction in each of the three areas.

On-the-Spot Differentiation

When teachers differentiate *on the spot*, they do so because, in the midst of teaching, they see an opportunity to help a child or a group of children learn *better*. The example from Christian's classroom shows a weather center that is set up for *all* of the children to explore general elements of the curriculum: maps, weather, reading, and writing. However, as we will see, many possibilities are present for on-the-spot differentiating: for tailoring the *instructional support*, the *materials and activities*, and the *logistics* to connect with individual children's strengths and needs.

Instructional support

The work that Christian does with Jake and his thinking about Canada and Mexico is one example of on-the-spot *instructional support*. Christian watches to see what he knows and then responds to his thinking. A differentiating teacher responds to what individual children are doing and thinking at the moment, providing instruction that helps them expand their thinking in a direction that is relevant to *them*.

With this in mind, on any given day in the weather center, we can expect for Christian to purposefully support individuals in varied ways. On one day, she might stop to listen to one of the advanced readers read a Web-based weather report, helping the child use and develop specific reading strategies as the potential arises. On another day, she might support a less advanced reader by taking dictation of a report and then listening to the child read it back to her. On another day, she may sit down and support several children as they invent spellings to write their reports, or she may give an impromptu lesson on something like using a spelling strategy to change weather-word nouns (*rain, wind, cloud*) into weather-word adjectives (*rainy, windy, cloudy*).

Jotting down quick notes helps Christian remember if there is a particular strategy or area of understanding with which a child or group of children may need additional support. But the primary goal of on-the-spot instructional differentiation is to spontaneously capture as many teachable moments as possible.

Materials and activities

Teachers also watch for ways to differentiate center *materials and activities* on the spot. As we saw in the example, after observing in the weather center, Christian encouraged some of the children (the more advanced readers) to use the weather reports on the Internet instead of using the material that was already in the center. A differentiating teacher tunes in to how well and how deeply children are engaging with materials and activities and makes adjustments accordingly.

With this in mind, on any given day in this center, we might find Christian adding or removing reading materials, finding a book for an individual who has taken a special interest in a topic, or simplifying or enhancing an activity for a child. The goal of on-the-spot differentiation of materials and activities is to keep each child interested and appropriately challenged throughout the center period.

Logistics

Finally, teachers engage in on-the-spot differentiation of *logistics*—procedures related to the working environment and the time frame for activities. For example, after observing in the weather center, we might expect for Christian to suggest to a child who is slow to get started (as Grace was) that she write her report in a private or quiet area of the classroom, perhaps with one other child. The weather center is turning out to be one of the more lively, talk-filled centers in the classroom, and some children are less than productive when they work here. Another option, depending on what Christian knows about Grace, is to encourage her to continue her work here even after the other children

Differentiating Center Experiences on the Spot and Through Structured Planning

Differentiating the Support

- Be available to provide on-the-spot, individualized support during center time.
- Meet with children before center time to provide extra modeling or to help them get started on an activity so that they may successfully complete it later.
- For reading-based activities, meet with a group beforehand to provide instruction that will enable successful reading later. For example, build background knowledge by discussing what the piece is about, read the piece to the group, or provide a graphic organizer that will help the children get the gist of the piece. For bilingual or English language learners, read very expressively, use gestures and facial expressions, and help with making connections between illustrations and words. If possible, provide opportunities for children to discuss the material in their strong language.
- Arrange for an older student or parent volunteer to work with children at the center. Volunteers may provide support with instructions or reading, read materials aloud, support children's writing, or take dictation for writing (if assigned by you).
- Provide a partner with whom to complete certain activities.
- Assign a peer to provide support with instructions, reading, or writing.
- For reading-based activities, arrange for a member of the center group to read the material aloud.
- Create individual instruction sheets for (or with) students, or place an instruction sheet at a center even if only a few children are likely to use it.
- For students receiving special services, collaborate with the teacher to arrange for the children to receive support with some center activities.
- Send an activity home so parents can help the child get started early.
- For bilingual or English language learners, arrange for center-based instructional support in the native language. This may involve arranging for an aide or a volunteer adult with whom to read a text, discuss its content, discuss instructions, preview a text, respond to a piece of literature, and so on.

Differentiating the Materials and Activities

- Monitor how well the materials and activities are working for the children. Make on-the-spot adaptations and suggestions as appropriate.
- Offer choices of activities, allowing students to differentiate for themselves.
- Offer choices of learning materials. Ensure that materials reflect a variety of topics, interests, languages, and cultures.
- Provide reading materials written at varied levels of difficulty but with similar content. Support children in finding the appropriate material.

Figure 5–1 *Differentiating Center Experiences*

- Offer reading material on tape.
- Vary the amount of reading that is necessary to complete an activity.
- Alter graphic organizers or worksheets in order to challenge each child appropriately.
- Instead of requiring writing, allow for audiotaping, drawing, or sculpting.
- Instead of requiring writing, arrange for an aide or adult volunteer to take dictation.
- Arrange for the student to type written work.
- Vary the amount of writing that is necessary to complete an activity.
- Talk with individual students about goals and expectations for center work; vary as appropriate, keeping in mind that the goal for all children is to expand from where they are currently.
- Accept different ways of expressing knowledge: writing, speaking, typing, drawing, creating an exhibit.
- For bilingual or English language learners, arrange for students to read, write, listen to, and discuss literature in both languages.

Differentiating the Logistics
- Regularly monitor how well the environmental and social conditions are supporting children's learning. Make adjustments as appropriate.
- Offer the child more time to complete an activity.
- Offer the child time before center time to get started on an activity.
- Offer the child time after center time to complete an activity.
- Arrange for the child to skip one center in order to have time to complete activities at another center.
- Purposefully place a child in a group based on how well he or she will work with the other children in that group.
- Vary the number of students per group.
- Offer choices in terms of where to work in the classroom.
- Allow the child to work in a quiet, private, or soft area, with another child if appropriate.
- Offer choices in terms of with whom to work.
- Provide alternative seating or create standing space in various centers.
- Allow the child to move around while completing an activity.
- Offer a variety of mini-environments in the classroom (peaceful, active, dimly lit, lamp-lit, room for movement, soft music, etc.).
- Offer students opportunities to work and speak in their native languages with other children who speak the same language.

Figure 5–1 *Continued*

move on. It may be that Grace is one of those children who benefits from using talk—lots of it—as a form of rehearsal for writing.

A differentiating teacher is aware that children work differently and at different paces and therefore benefit when they are not all treated the same. Any child may require more time to complete an activity, a different environment for completing it, or an altered social situation in which to work. The goal of differentiating logistics on the spot is to continually fine-tune each child's experience, to work to cultivate conditions that allow each child to work fruitfully, comfortably, and within a time frame that is individually realistic.

Structured Differentiation

Along with on-the-spot efforts, teachers use center time to differentiate in more *structured*, planned ways. To do so, they typically pull together *groups* of children who will benefit from *similar* kinds of support, or they single out *individual* students who will benefit from preplanned support.

Unfortunately, some teachers engage in structured differentiation *only* as they work with readers, *only* in guided reading groups, using *only* one major criterion for differentiation: the level of text that the children can read with relatively few errors. This is not enough. Although text-level grouping can be useful for decoding instruction, especially when children are just beginning to decode, as we will see, all three forms of differentiation—used in varied ways—are logical and beneficial during center time.

Instructional support

Structured instructional support during center time often occurs in the form of individual or small-group minilessons that are focused on a particular writing or reading strategy. For example, a teacher might pull together a group to work on a spelling strategy such as inventing, adding -*ed* endings, or choosing between -*at* and -*ate*. Or, he may pull aside an individual who has been observed to take no spelling risks and help her begin to generate some invented spellings. The goal of structured differentiation is to ensure that each child receives thoughtful strategy lessons that are tailored to his or her individual needs.

Materials and activities

Often in combination with planning for differentiated instructional support, teachers plan for children to engage with differentiated materials and activities.

Probably the most common reason for an early childhood teacher to differentiate materials during center time is to individualize small-group reading instruction. (As described in Chapter 4, small-group reading instruction often occurs during center time.) Small groups that are formed based on text difficulty enable teachers to instruct children using material that is written at an optimal level for the development of word identification (decoding) strategies. Many sources suggest that material that a child can read with an accuracy level of about 90 percent is optimal for such instruction. That is, if a child miscues on about ten words in one hundred, then using that piece as instructional material is likely to best support the development of word identification strategies. (Because miscues vary in quality, consider this a very general rule of thumb.) Along with reading particular texts with *small groups*, teachers often plan for children to use particular (or leveled) texts *for partner reading* or *independent reading* during center time.

Of course, children's *experiences* and *interests* are other important issues to consider when planning for differentiation of materials and activities. When children are interested and connected, they are most likely to stretch themselves into new ways of thinking. Therefore, during center time, students benefit when you differentiate by offering individual choices of what to read, write, and inquire into and choices of ways to demonstrate their knowledge. Or, if you know that a child is interested in basketball or boats or Disney or deer, differentiate by seeking out related materials and making them available when possible.

In addition to differentiating materials, give children choices in how to demonstrate their knowledge about them. For example, a retelling or a critique could be accomplished through writing but also through talking or drawing.

Along with arranging for *individual* choice, you may wish to arrange for students to form or be placed in *groups* to work on projects and activities. For example, the first center of the day could be a time for special-topic groups to meet. Or children could travel from center to center with partners who have similar interests.

As you consider materials and activities, keep in mind that each child needs to be able to successfully *complete* center activities. For some, this will mean that you provide special materials or alter the assignment in some way. However, if you plan for lots of open-ended activities and choices, much of the differentiation will naturally be enacted by the children themselves.

When we require that all children engage with the same materials and the same activities, some end up in situations that rarely allow for them to be successful. The ultimate goal of structured differentiation of materials and activities is to ensure that each child has extensive, in-depth opportunities to engage with learning in ways that they find interesting, personally relevant, and appropriately challenging. Center time should be a time for all children to be successful.

Logistics

Finally, children benefit when teachers make plans for differentiating *logistics*. Deliberately altering the social and physical environment, and the time frame, for activities can make a tremendous difference in how successful some children will be.

To differentiate logistics, as you form groups, you may wish to place children together strategically. Some teachers purposefully group children together who work well together. Some explore what happens when they place talkative children with other talkative children or less talkative children with other less talkative children. Some teachers prefer allowing children to choose with whom to work. Some group children so that they have frequent opportunities to work with others in their native language. Carefully observing groups in action will give you the information that you need to best support children as they work in collaborative situations.

Inevitably, you will have students who work better in different areas of the classroom. Some may seem to accomplish more, or work more peaceably, within a quieter area or in a private area. Some may prefer an area that allows for a bit more movement. A few Monday-morning conferences with these children could help you make a plan for each to spend some work time in his or her favored areas.

You probably also have students who regularly need extra time to complete activities. This may be because they work slowly or because they leave the classroom during center time for special services. You might build into your schedule a period of time to pull together these students, allowing them to get started early or to finish up later. Or you might develop a plan for these children to work in one or two centers instead of two or three. The ultimate goal in planning for differentiated logistics is to ensure working conditions and time frames that realistically connect with each child's needs.

As you think through the different ways of differentiating instruction, you may find it helpful to organize your plans on a chart. Figure 5–2 shows a filled-out example of a planning worksheet that may be used to organize for differentiated instruction. A blank worksheet can be found in Chapter 4 (Figure 4–13). Other forms for organizing differentiation can be found later in this chapter.

Child's Name	Centers Needing Accommodations	Other Support
Lucy	*Center 1:* Work with partner (Jessica). *Center 8:* Use puppets in private area with one other student (instead of in puppet theatre).	*Daily Goal Sheet:* 1. Use only kind words. 2. Use words rather than grabbing or pushing.
Shane	*Center 1:* Work with partner (Tomas). *Center 7:* Use simplified graphic organizer.	• Work on language for requesting help from other children. • Use MWF choice times to get started on center activities.
Jamal		*Daily Goal Sheet:* 1. Complete top-quality work at each center. 2. Complete activity before moving on to next center.
Monica	*Center 1:* Work with partner (Frannie). *Center 3:* Draw retelling. *Center 6:* Dictate story. *Center 7:* Use simplified graphic organizer.	• Use MWF choice times to get started on center activities.
Anthony	*Center 6:* Dictate story.	
Noel		• Use MWF choice times to get started on center activities.

Figure 5-2 *Organizing for Differentiated Instruction Example*

The Child's Role

As you plan, keep in mind that teachers are not the only ones who make the important decisions about differentiation. In fact, the *children's* decisions about differentiation are just as critical to the success of center activities as are the teacher's.

To allow for children to differentiate for themselves, give them opportunities to make as many of their own choices as possible. For example, you may encourage your students to choose to work independently or with others; choose one activity from a set of three; select their own reading materials; choose what to write about; lead an activity; or make some of their own decisions about logistics. These processes will naturally support your efforts in working toward experiences that are meaningful and engaging for each child and will also encourage children's developing independence in identifying and making use of their learning strengths and preferences. The different center models described in Chapter 4 leave room for building in opportunities for student choice.

Center Time Assessment

By now it is apparent that differentiating instruction requires careful assessment. Teachers need assessment information to make decisions about how to differentiate—about how to group children for instruction, about the specific kinds of support and information they need, and about the kinds of materials and activities that will allow for them to expand their concepts and thinking.

Center time may be used to document and assess in areas that you *typically* assess. For example, if you regularly collect information about how children comprehend, or the strategies they use to decode, or the development of their writing, then center time can be used to gather that information. You may gather it as you meet with groups or individuals. You can purposefully design centers to suit your specific assessment needs, or you could just grab a clipboard and go to the centers, where children are likely to be engaged in activities that will help you understand their needs.

Figures 5–3 through 5–6 offer examples of assessment activities and instructional planning forms that you may adapt for your own use during center time and as you plan for differentiated instruction. You will notice that the assessments are directly connected with the literacy goals described in Chapter 2.

Long-Term Monitoring of Center Activities

As with any assessment you do, center time assessment focuses on collecting work samples and other forms of documentation that will inform your instruction and show evidence of children's growth over time. Keeping the information in a work folder or portfolio facilitates this process.

You might wish to distinguish between a weekly work folder, in which children temporarily store center activities, and a more long-term literacy portfolio that allows you and your students to track growth over time. The work folder can be used to monitor children's weekly activity and as a place to store material that will be shared with the class. The long-term portfolio could be used to store pieces that will give you more extensive ideas for instruction and that could be used to reflect on the child's long-term growth and goals. Three possible categories for organizing a long-term portfolio follow:

1. *sociocultural knowledge and experience* (projects, list of child's interests, notes from interviews or conferences, anecdotal notes)

2. *reading growth* (reading samples, list of preferred genres and topics, list of materials read, retellings, illustrated reflections, notes from reading interviews or conferences, self-evaluations, anecdotal notes)

3. *writing* (writing samples, list of preferred genres and topics, list of pieces written, spelling evaluations, self-evaluations, anecdotal notes)

All children can be expected to do high-quality work in centers—work that teaches, engages, and encourages new ways of thinking. The role of differentiation in all of the ways described in this chapter is to help ensure that this happens.

Figure 5–3a *Observe a Read-Aloud*

Read-Aloud Observation

Child's Name: _____ Date: _____

Text: _____ Text Level if Known: _____

1. Make a copy of a complete text. As you listen to the student read the original, either to you or the center group, use the copy to document miscues and make notes about reading conduct (such as asking for help, commenting on content, asking a question, expressing confusion, or hesitating extensively).

2. When the student is finished reading, request a retelling, and take note of the key ideas expressed.

3. Evaluate the *patterns of miscues* and *reading conduct* to determine whether the student would benefit from individual or group instruction in using any of the following text-processing strategies and knowledge:

   ____ monitoring meaning

   ____ using prior knowledge and cues in text to predict words and phrases

   ____ using phonics knowledge and the developing context to help identify words, and cross-checking to be sure that what is read makes sense

   ____ self-correcting miscues that do not make sense

   ____ omitting words or substituting words to keep reading

   ____ using illustrations and pictures selectively

   ____ automatically identifying words

   ____ using fix-up strategies (rereading, reading on, slowing down, checking punctuation, identifying the confusing words)

4. Evaluate the retelling to determine whether the student needs support with capturing the *gist* and the key *details* of a piece. Record ideas for individual or group support.

Organizing Differentiated Instruction Based on Read-Alouds

Make a copy of a complete text. As you listen to the student read the original, either to you or to the center group, use the copy to document miscues and make notes about reading conduct (such as asking for help, commenting on content, asking a question, expressing confusion, or hesitating extensively). When the student is finished reading, request a retelling, and take note of the key ideas expressed.

Evaluate the *patterns of miscues, reading conduct,* and *retelling* to determine whether the student would benefit from individual or group instruction on any of items listed below. Place a check in the appropriate boxes to indicate such need, and group students accordingly.

Students' Names	Monitor meaning	Predict	Use phonics and context	Self-correct	Omit or substitute	Use pictures and illustrations	Automatic identification	Fix-up strategies	Retelling/ comprehension

Figure 5–4a *Observe a Retelling*

Retelling Observation

Child's Name: _____ Date: _____

Text: _____ Text Level if Known: _____

1. Observe a child's retelling of a piece that he or she has listened to or read. The child may retell orally to you or the center group, or the child may write, draw, or use a graphic organizer. Take note of the key ideas and details expressed.

   ____ Are key events or ideas included?

   ____ Are important or interesting details included?

   ____ Is the sequence of the retelling logical?

   ____ Is there evidence that the child is making inferences and thinking beyond the text?

   ____ Is something important missing? Jot it down:

2. Record ideas for individual or group instruction:

Figure 5–4b *Organizing Differentiated Instruction Based on Retellings*

Organizing Differentiated Instruction Based on Retellings

Observe a child's retelling of a piece that he or she has listened to or read. The child may retell orally, or write, draw, or use a graphic organizer. Take note of the key ideas and details expressed. Place a check in the appropriate boxes to indicate a need for instruction and group students accordingly.

Students' Names	Key events or ideas	Important or interesting details	Logical sequence	Evidence for inferences/thinking beyond the text	What are the missing ideas?

Having a Reading Conference

Talk Together

Ask questions such as the following:

- What do you think about and pay attention to when you are reading?
- How are you feeling about your reading? Why?
- What is hard for you when you read?
- What is easy?
- What do you do when you are reading and you get stuck?
- What do you do when you are reading but you don't understand?
- What kinds of things do you like to read?

Listen Together

- Listen to a very short recording of a student reading. Discuss the miscues and why they were made.
- Listen to a recording of a student retelling a piece. Discuss strengths and what could be added.

Analyze Together

Listen to a student (or students in a group) read a short piece aloud. Stop occasionally to discuss meaning-making and text-processing strategies. For example:

- Did you make any connections here? How does connecting help you as a reader?
- I noticed that when you got stuck, you backed up and reread. That's a helpful strategy when you are losing meaning.
- You didn't know how to read this word, so you tried and then skipped it. If you needed to know it, what else could you try?

Strategize Together

Talk about next steps:

- What goals should we set for you?
- What can I do to help you with your reading?
- Is there something you could do at home to help?
- Is there a particular topic that you would like to read about?

Figure 5–5 *Have a Reading Conference: Possible Directions for Individuals or Groups*

Figure 5–6a *Observe as the Child Writes*

Writing Observation

Child's Name: _____ Date: _____

Title: _____ Genre: _____

1. Observe the child in a natural setting for writing.

2. Evaluate the child's writing processes:

   What does the child do well?

   What is difficult or in need of instruction?

3. Record ideas for individual or group instruction:

Figure 5–6b *Writing Conference Check Sheet*

Writing Conference

1. In collaboration with the child, regularly collect samples of writing. For the conference, choose a series of the samples (three or four taken at least a week apart).

2. Together, review the child's strengths, needs, and progress, consulting items from the checklist below as appropriate.

   _____ Uses writing to serve multiple functions; writes about a range of topics; chooses own topics.

   _____ Develops rich content in writing.

   _____ Uses varied resources to locate information (other children, reference books, pictionaries, the Internet).

   _____ Invents spellings, using progressively more sophisticated phonics knowledge; conventionally spells an increasing number of commonly used words.

   _____ Uses punctuation and capitalization.

   _____ Proofreads, revises, and edits as appropriate.

   _____ Uses different voices; uses vocabulary, grammatical forms, and genres appropriate to goals.

3. Set one or two writing goals together:

4. Record ideas for individual or group instruction:

Figure 5–6c *Organizing Differentiated Instruction Based on Writing*

Organizing Differentiated Instruction Based on Writing

Based on your conferences with students and/or observations of their writing, place a check in the appropriate boxes to indicate a need for instruction. Group students accordingly.

Students' Names	Writes about range of topics	Chooses own topics	Develop rich content	Uses varied resources	Spelling strategies (indicate which)	Punctuation and capitalization (indicate which)	Proofing, revising, editing	Voice	Vocabulary	Grammar

CHAPTER 6

The Centers

In today's classrooms, literacy centers do much more than keep children occupied so that the teacher has time to work with small groups of readers. Today's literacy centers are carefully designed to deeply engage children in learning and to support them in advancing all aspects of their literacy knowledge.

This chapter offers a set of center ideas that may be used in kindergarten through third-grade classrooms. As with any teaching ideas, as you implement these centers, I recommend that you carefully observe your students to determine the specific kinds of adaptations and differentiation that will ensure their interest, edification, and success.

Although the centers are presented in seven sections that reflect the seven literacy goals described in Chapter 2, most of the centers actually emphasize several competencies at once. For example, a center that emphasizes *book handling* might also emphasize *comprehension*, while a center that emphasizes *writing* might also emphasize *vocabulary* and *sociocultural knowledge*. In addition, although all of the centers are focused on achieving language and literacy goals, many of the activities could easily be integrated with content area goals.

Index of Centers

Sociocultural Practice Centers

- Family Tales
- Kid Tales
- Family Literacy Materials
- Family Literacy
- Recreation
- Homework Talk

- Greeting Cards
- Job Play
- Family Design

Book-Handling and Book-Sharing Centers

- Listen and Share
- Partner Reading
- Book Discussion
- Book Making
- Book Talks
- Teacher Play

Comprehension and Meaning-Making Centers

- Reading
- Drama and Retelling
- Literature Response
- Poetry
- Information Gathering
- Story Endings
- Sequencing
- Toy Company Play
- We Design: Digging In

Word Reading and Spelling Centers

- Special Library
- Word Puzzles and Games
- Alphabet Book Writing
- Alphabet Book Reading
- Letter and Word Study
- Word Hunts
- We Design: Reading

Fluency Centers

- Listening
- Readers Theatre
- Audiotaping
- Language Transcription
- Expressive Reading
- Big Books
- News Play

Writing Centers

- Drafting, Revising, and Editing
- Publishing
- Note to Someone
- Message Writing

- Observation
- Post Office Play

- We Design: Writing

Vocabulary Centers

- Story Sharing
- Word Exchange
- All the Words You Can Think Of

- Vocabulary Study
- Text Sets
- Author and Book Publisher Play

Sociocultural Practice

Family Tales

Materials

Tape recorders; five- to ten-minute cassette recordings made by family members; materials for writing

Possible activities

- Students listen to stories and information recorded by family members. (Just one recording is needed to get this center started.) After listening, they prepare a response. For example:

  - Write about something you learned.

  - Write about something you found interesting.

  - Draw a picture that illustrates what you heard.

- Students listen to stories and information recorded by family members. After listening, they write a note to thank a family member for contributing to the project. In the note, they tell about something they found interesting or something they learned.

Preparation and instruction

- Acquaint families with this project by sending a note home, or arrange to acquaint them with the project at conferences.

■ Supply each family with a short, labeled cassette tape to be used for recording a story. As needed, allow families to borrow a tape recorder (or come in to the school to record). Recordings may include

- a favorite story read or told by a family member

- a story about the student when he or she was younger

- a description of a family member's day (see Figure 6–1)

■ Show the class how to use the listening equipment.

Kid Tales

Materials

Tape recorder; cassette tapes for two- to four-minute recordings of scripts that students have written (or dictated); writing materials

Possible activities

■ *Week 1:* Children write (or dictate) short scripts about personal or family interests, traditions, or pastimes. If you help the class generate the ideas before center time, a parent volunteer can help with the writing (or dictation).

■ *Week 2 (optional):* When the children have completed their writing (or dictation) from week 1, plan a center for audiotaping the material. For children who are unable to read material that they have dictated, an adult should record it as they listen.

■ *Week 3 (optional):* When the material has been recorded, plan a listening center so that children can listen and respond to the stories and information recorded by other students. For example:

- Write about something new you learned.

- Write about something you found interesting.

- Draw a picture that illustrates what you heard.

- Create a web with your peer's name in the middle. Use the spokes to record (write or draw) what you have learned about this peer.

Figure 6–1 *Framework for Family Recording*

Framework for Family Recording

1. My name is . . .

2. I am a . . . [mom, dad, big brother, grandmother, chef, dry cleaner, musician, Spanish teacher, dentist, sheet metal worker, truck driver, dog, cat, pony]

3. One of the first things I do most days is . . .

4. One of the most important things I do during the day is . . .

5. The best part of my day is . . .

6. The hardest part of my day is . . .

7. One thing I do a lot during the day is . . .

8. I end the day by . . .

Preparation and instruction

Help students decide what to write about, and model your own writing about personal or family interests, traditions, or pastimes. Show the class how to use the recording and listening equipment.

Family Literacy Materials

Materials

Literacy materials brought from students' homes; materials for writing

Possible activities

Each student brings in one piece of print material from home. Possibilities include a storybook, an informational book, a recipe book, a cereal box, a note, a greeting card, a comic strip, information printed from a website, a short newspaper or magazine article, an advertisement, and a coupon. Students use center time to browse, read, and discuss the materials.

Preparation and instruction

Send a note home to explain the project to families.

Family Literacy

Materials

A variety of reading and writing materials, depending on the activity

Possible activities

Before the center period, students' family members share knowledge with or provide a demonstration for the whole class. After watching the demonstration, students use center time to read material related to the experience (such as books, instruction manuals, or food packages) and/or to write about the experience (what they learned, how they felt about the experience, a thank-you note, instructions, a related story).

Preparation and instruction

Arrange for families to visit and share (see Figure 6–2). Work with family members to determine the kinds of follow-up reading and writing that might be appropriate.

Family Literacy

To help make this school year meaningful for each child, I would like to invite a member of each family to come to the classroom and share a bit of expertise with us. The children will follow up by talking, reading, and writing about the experience, and it will become a part of our literacy curriculum. Good times to visit are Monday mornings and Friday afternoons, but if this is not possible, accommodations will be made.

   What knowledge, guidance, or experiences would you like to offer to the classroom?

_____ Bring in a story to read.

_____ Tell a story (personal, family, community, traditional, folktale).

_____ Sing a song or play a musical instrument.

_____ Provide a demonstration (groom a pet, feed a baby, decorate a cake, make a quilt block, braid someone's hair, show how a tractor works).

_____ Share hobbies or work-related knowledge such as cooking, painting, car detailing, gardening, fishing, sewing, woodworking, secretarial, retail, health, and so on.

_____ Share an object of interest.

_____ Teach students to play a game.

_____ Teach something about the language that you speak.

_____ Other _____

If you would like to come but aren't sure what you would like do, please call or email!

Name: _____

Possible days and times to visit: _____

Figure 6–2 *Family Literacy: Letter to Parents*

Recreation

Materials

Reading materials that support students' personal interests and pastimes (have students help you pull together this material)

Possible activities

- Students browse and read the materials, talking with their center group about their interests. Then they draw a picture of something that represents one of their interests.

- *Week 1:* Students browse the materials until they find a topic that interests them. Then they use the materials to write a personal narrative about the topic. For example, they might begin with

  - An interesting tradition in my family . . .

  - One of my favorite things to do . . .

  - Something I would like to learn . . .

- *Week 2 (optional):* After drafting a personal narrative, the student revises and edits it and then recopies it so that it may be used as one page in a class book. The student can illustrate it if he or she wishes.

Preparation and instruction

Collect a set of materials that ultimately reflects at least one personal interest of every child in your class. Families may be encouraged to loan materials for a period of time. Model the personal narrative style of writing for your students, and model revision and editing as it is appropriate to the students in your class.

Homework Talk

Materials

Half-sheets of paper (for homework); materials for writing

Possible activities

Have groups discuss family responses to homework questions. If relevant, they can graph the responses or compile the information using charts or webs. Examples of homework questions:

- Who is one important person in our family? Why is this person important?

- What is an important tradition in our family?

- How many languages are the members of my household able to speak?

- What are our favorite foods?

- How far do we live from the school?

- Has anyone in my family ever seen _____? [Give several choices, for example a coyote, a freshwater clam, an animal classified as endangered, an eclipse, a famous person, a parade, or a famous painting.] Tell about one of those times.

- What is a special place that our family has visited?

- What kind of print (newspaper, books, food packages, job-related material, etc.) does each family member read the most?

- What kind of writing (notes, work-related, lists, etc.) does each family member do the most?

Preparation and instruction

As homework, students bring home a designated question to discuss with family members and then bring back a response to discuss during center time. Develop the questions with your students, and when possible, see that they relate to the content area curriculum and inquiries in your classroom. Questions may be written or copied on a half-sheet of paper or photocopied. If some students do not bring the responses back, allow them to participate by developing their own responses. When relevant, organize the information on a graph as a class.

Greeting Cards

Materials

Sturdy paper; envelopes; colored pencils; markers; art materials

Possible activities

- Students create a variety of greeting cards (thank you, congratulations, birthday, holidays, welcome, thinking of you). As a class or a center team, children prepare packs of greeting cards to give as gifts. For example, they could give a pack to a lunch worker, a music teacher, the school principal, the secretary, a parent volunteer, a guest speaker, and so on.

- Children use student-created cards to prepare special greetings for friends and family. If desired, they can put the cards in labeled envelopes.

Preparation and instruction

Demonstrate any art or craft techniques that will be used to make the cards. For example, paintbrush strokes, etching techniques, or lift-the-flap structures might be appropriate. Discuss the kinds of greetings that cards typically contain, and discuss the information that is typically included when filling out envelopes.

Job Play

Materials

Items, including literacy materials, needed to play in a variety of job roles such as restaurant workers, office workers, store workers, school personnel, journalists, reporters, teachers, toy industry workers, actors, directors, and producers

Possible activities

Allow children to set the course for their own job play.

Preparation and instruction

As a whole class, decide on some possible play themes for the center. Focus on job roles. Make a list of items, including literacy materials, that would be needed to play in those roles. For example, a group playing as actors might wish to play with costumes, masks, scripts, and materials for writing scripts. Collect the materials and place them in the center.

Family Design

Materials

Any materials from the classroom may be used. Some materials from homes may be incorporated.

Possible activities

Over the course of the school year, design one center with each student and/or the student's family. The center should reflect a student interest, hobby, tradition, or pastime. You could implement one or two such centers per week. Examples of student- and family-created centers follow:

■ A family member brings in a hammer dulcimer and sheets of music. Students in the center play the dulcimer and talk about how to read music.

■ A family member brings in a fairy tale and reads it to students in the center. Students follow up by drawing a picture of the setting or the characters.

■ A family member demonstrates how to make a gingerbread house and students make minihouses.

■ A family member demonstrates how to make coffee-can ice cream and student groups make their own ice cream.

■ A student collects a set of library books focused on basketball, and the other students read through the books, looking for and writing down interesting facts. The material is compiled into a book of facts about basketball.

■ A student writes about a favorite holiday or family event and uses the writing as a model for other students to write about a favorite holiday or family event. Later you can compile the material into a class book.

Preparation and instruction

Discuss possibilities for designing the centers. Have the student sketch out a plan for his or her center and give appropriate feedback. If family members are to be involved, send home a note describing the process (see Figure 6–2). Develop a calendar that can be used to organize the implementation of the child- or family-designed centers.

Book Handling and Sharing

Listen and Share

Materials

Picture books (fiction and nonfiction); tape containing the following script

Possible activities

Students work in teams to follow a set of directions that emphasize book-handling and book-sharing competencies.

Preparation and instruction

Make a tape recording of the following script (or a script that is relevant to your students' book-handling and book-sharing needs).

1. Hold the book so that both of you can see the front cover.

2. Point to the title. Read it aloud.

3. Point to the author's name. Read it aloud.

4. Look at the picture on the cover and talk about the information that it gives you. *Stop the tape until you are finished talking.*

5. Look at the back cover. Talk about what you see there. *Stop the tape until you are finished talking.*

6. Open the book and turn to where the text begins. Get ready to read the book. When you are finished reading, turn back through all of the pages, telling your partner at least one thing you liked or found interesting. *Stop the tape and rewind it.*

   or

   Turn through the pages, looking at each picture. When you are finished reading, turn back through all of the pages, telling your partner at least one thing you liked or found interesting. *Stop the tape and rewind it.*

To prepare students for the activity, play the tape, and with one student as your partner, model the process for the whole class. Show students how to stop the tape to give themselves time to talk and to then start it up again to listen for the next instructions. The tape may be used with fiction or nonfiction.

Partner Reading

Materials

High-interest books; comfortable seating for pairs

Possible activities

■ Partners take turns reading aloud. One partner could read an entire book, and then the other partner could read a different book. Or the partners could switch halfway through one book. Or plan for students who need a little extra support to read the *same* book after their partner has read it. After reading, partners choose from the following:

• Discuss what you found interesting.

• Retell what you have read.

Preparation and instruction

■ Model how to choose a book, especially if you would like for students to read texts written at particular levels of difficulty or complexity.

■ Model different options for the reading (as described previously).

■ Model how to support a reader who gets stuck on a word.

■ Model what to do if the selected literature is too difficult.

■ Model how to present an interesting or thorough retelling (see Figures 6–10 and 6–11).

Book Discussion

Materials

High-interest books (big books may be used); large paper

Possible activities

One student reads a book to the group (or the teacher reads to the whole class before center time). Then, the reader or a different student leads a follow-up discussion. The discussion may be open-ended or the student may use a discussion starter such as the following:

■ What parts did you like?

■ What did you think of this book?

■ Which character was most interesting to you?

■ What is one thing you learned from this book?

Option: After reading and talking, students work together to create a joint response that incorporates the content of their discussion. For example, they may construct a list of the parts they liked, write a general response to the content, draw the characters they thought were most interesting, or web the things they learned from the book. (For an extensive list of response possibilities, see Figure 6–12.)

Preparation and instruction

Form a small group to model the procedures that you would like your students to follow. Help students understand how to ensure that each group member has a turn to respond to the literature and that all ideas are included in any written or drawn response that the group prepares.

Materials

Pencils; crayons; paper; staplers; glue; tape; pictionaries or dictionaries; a variety of materials for making books

Possible activities

■ Students make a book about something that the class is studying.

■ Students make a book about a topic of personal interest.

■ Students make an *All About* _____ book.

■ Students write a story and turn it into a book.

■ Students make a book of poetry. They can write their own poems and/or copy poems that they like.

Preparation and instruction

Model how to put together a book by writing the pages first and then stapling them together in the preferred order. Show children how to create unique books containing pop-ups, textures, or flaps.

Book Talks

Materials

Books; book talk planning forms

Possible activities

■ Students draw a picture in preparation to give a book talk to the class at the end of center time (see Figure 6–3).

■ Students write in preparation to give a book talk to the class at the end of center time (see Figure 6–4).

Preparation and instruction

Read a book aloud to the class and then model a book talk using one of the planning forms.

Figure 6–3 *Book Talk Picture Form*

Book Talk Picture Form

Name: _____

Book: _____

Draw a picture of something you liked about the book and use it to give a book talk.

Figure 6–4 *Book Talk Writing Form*

Book Talk Writing Form

Name: _____

Title of Book: _____

Opening line for book talk: _____

_____

_____

_____

What the book is about: _____

_____

_____

_____

What you liked about the book: _____

_____

_____

_____

Closing line: _____

_____

_____

_____

Teacher Play

Materials

Locate this center in the area that you use to do whole-group instruction. Allow students to use an easel, big books and a pointer, chart paper and a marker, small books, and any other instructional material that you use as you instruct.

Possible activities

- Allow children to develop their own play scenarios, acting as teachers, students, and any other school-related roles of their choosing.

- Encourage children to play as teacher at the easel, with one child leading a book sharing or shared writing session while others act as students.

- Provide a set of small books so that children can play at small-group instruction.

Preparation and instruction

Show students the materials available for play and discuss possible play roles.

Comprehension and Meaning Making

Reading

Materials

Comfortable seating; books from the class library organized in a neat display

Possible activities

- Students independently read books of choice.

- Students independently reread a book they have already read or listened to during small- or whole-group instruction.

- Students pair up and read together.

- Students choose one member of the center group to read a book aloud.

Preparation and instruction

Clarify expectations for reading in this center.

Drama and Retelling

Materials

Familiar, favorite books; retelling tools (puppets, props, dry-erase board, graphic organizers)

Possible activities

- Students retell using puppets.

- Students retell using the materials in a prop box. A prop box contains a book and any characters or props that might be used to retell the story or the information.

- Students retell using a dry-erase board.

- Students retell using a graphic organizer. (See Figures 6–5 to 6–9 for reproducible forms.)

Preparation and instruction

Model how to use retelling tools such as puppets, props, and graphic organizers, and model and discuss what to include in a retelling. Although there are no hard rules for what to include, it may help to work from a list of suggestions. Figures 6–10 and 6–11 offer some possibilities. Consider setting each child up with a partner so that students will have an audience to retell to after they have prepared a retelling, or arrange for the center group to leave the last few minutes of the center session open to hear the retelling.

Literature Response

Materials

Varied literature (fiction, nonfiction, poetry) selected by the teacher or students

Possible activities

Students use drawing or writing to respond to literature that you have read to the class or that groups, partners, or individuals have read during center time. On any given day, response possibilities may be open-ended, you may assign a response, or you may provide students with a set of choices. Figure 6–12 offers a set of ideas to help you get literature response going. Encourage students to discuss their responses as they work.

Figure 6–5 *Story Sequencing Map*

Story Sequencing Map

Title: _____

Beginning

Middle

End

Figure 6–6 *General Story Map*

General Story Map

Title: _____

Characters	Setting

Problem	Resolution

Figure 6–7 *Detailed Story Map*

Detailed Story Map

Title: _____

Characters and Setting

Events (draw lines to make as many boxes as you need)

Theme

Figure 6–8 *Informational Text Map*

Name: _____ Date: _____

Title: _____ Pages: _____

Why I Read This Book: _____

Short Description or Drawing of the Important Ideas or Events

1.

2.

3.

4.

© 2005 Gretchen Owocki from *Time for Literacy Centers*. Portsmouth, NH: Heinemann.

Figure 6–9 *Information Web*

Place a key idea or word in the middle and supporting details or examples or characteristics around the spokes.

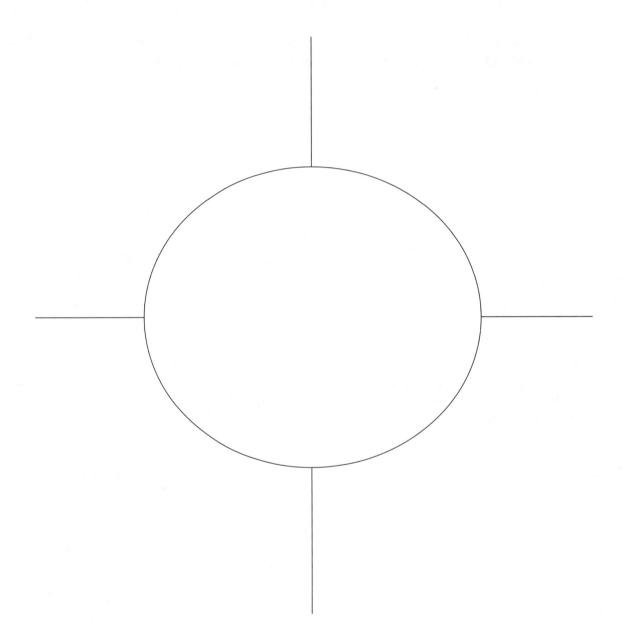

Figure 6–10 *Retelling Stories Guidelines*

Retelling Stories

- title and author

- important characters

- setting

- problem or goal

- events

- resolution

- theme

Figure 6–11 *Retelling Informational Text Guidelines*

Retelling Informational Text

- title and author

- topic and setting

- how text is organized

- important ideas, information, or events

- why you read this

- why author wrote this

Literature Response Possibilities

Respond to a piece of literature by drawing or writing about the following:

- something that you found interesting (tell why)
- something that surprised you (tell why)
- a favorite part (tell why)
- a part you didn't like (tell why)
- a favorite character (tell why)
- a character you didn't like (tell why)
- what the main character or personality did at a certain point; what you would do in a similar situation (tell why)
- an alternative to a story resolution
- what you think about the illustrations (tell why)
- what you think about the story or information (tell why)
- one way you will use information from the text
- why you think the author wrote this text
- who you think should read this text (tell why)
- your goals for reading this text and whether they were met or not met
- a question you have
- a wondering you have
- something that you learned
- something that confused you
- your visual image of a character or personality
- your visual image of a character or personality at a particular point in time
- your visual image of a part of the setting
- your visual image of an event
- a personal connection
- a feeling you had while reading
- a character or personality with whom you particularly identified (see Figure 6–15)
- a connection between texts (see Figures 6–16, 6–17, and 6–18)
- something you are thinking or feeling now that you have read the text
- something that this text reminded you of
- an important quote or picture from the text (tell why it is important)

Or respond by creating one of the following:

- a record of interesting, new, or important words
- a diagram, picture, or model that shows what you have learned
- a book review
- a poster or advertisement to publicize the book
- a television commercial to publicize the book
- an evaluation form (see Figures 6–13 and 6–14 for examples)

Figure 6–12 *Literature Response Possibilities*

Preparation and instruction

Model varying ways to respond to literature through drawing or writing. Over time, create a list of response possibilities with your students and hang it in the center. Eventually, this list will help students independently choose a response type. Before opening up the choices to students, you may wish to assign specific responses so that you have a chance to model them.

Poetry

Materials

Poetry; materials for writing and illustrating

Possible activities

- Students read from a variety of poetry books. Then they share their favorites with the other students at the center.

- Students read or listen to a poem several times and visually represent it. They can choose from different media such as chalk, watercolors, colored pencils, crayons, and clay.

- Students read several poems and choose one favorite. Then they copy and illustrate the poem for a class anthology of favorites. (Include a favorite poem from the teacher!)

- Students write a free verse poem. Free verse poems are unrhymed and have no prescribed rhythm, format, or length.

- Students write a free verse poem about something that has made them happy or sad.

- Students write a free verse poem about something that they have seen in their neighborhood.

- Students write a free verse poem about a piece of professional art.

- Students create their own piece of art and then write a free verse poem about it.

- Students write a list poem. A list poem describes something in a list format. Items in the list may be single words, phrases, or sentences.

- Students write an acrostic poem. An acrostic poem begins with a topic that also functions as a title. Each letter of the title becomes the first letter of each line of the poem. Lines can be either a word or a phrase.

Figure 6–13 *Fiction Evaluation Form*

Good Fiction?

_____ Do the characters seem real?

_____ Is the story good?

_____ Does the author make you want to see what happens at the end?

_____ Are the illustrations interesting?

_____ Do the illustrations help you better understand the text?

Figure 6–14 *Nonfiction Evaluation Form*

Good Nonfiction?

_____ Is it easy to find information?

_____ Is the book interesting to children?

_____ Is the book easy to understand?

_____ Does the author make you care about the topic?

_____ Are the table of contents, headings, index, glossary, and illustrations helpful?

Figure 6–15 *Character/Personality Connections Map*

Character/Personality Connections

Book Title: _____

My Name: _____

Character or Personality Name: _____

Draw or write something about yourself.	Draw or write something about the character or personality you have chosen.

Describe the connection between yourself and the character or personality:

Figure 6–16 *Three-Column Comparison Chart*

Three-Column Comparison Chart

Topic: _____

Connection between _____ and _____

Information from Book 1:	Information from Book 2:	Both Books:

Figure 6-17 *Venn Diagram*

Topic: _____

Connection between _____ and _____

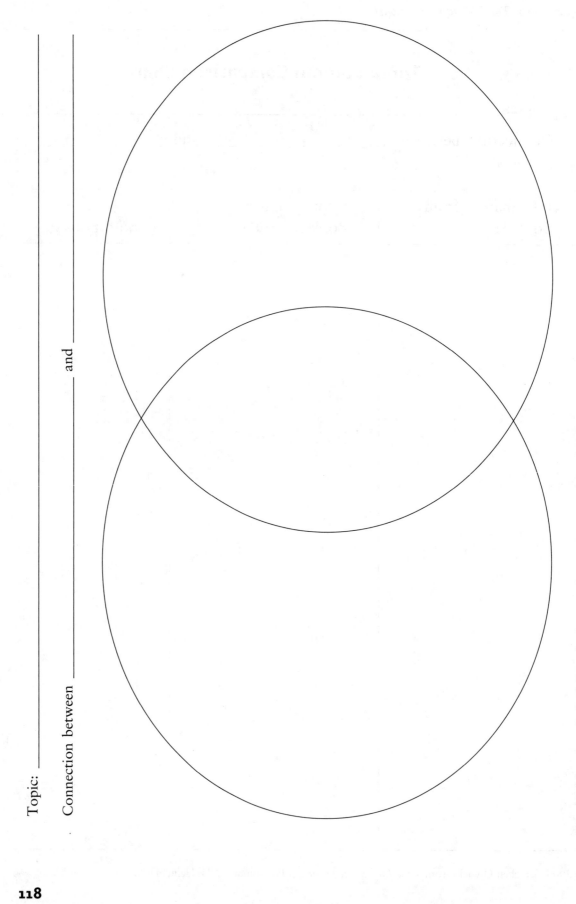

Figure 6–18 *Connections Between Texts Map*

Connections Between Texts

Name: _____

Book Title: _____

What I am comparing: _____

Draw or write something about one book's character, personality, setting, topic, theme, or author's style.	Draw or write something from another book that compares with what you have done in column 1.

Describe the connections between the two items:

■ Students write a haiku poem. Haiku poems typically portray a scene from nature and often include reference to a season. Haiku poems typically contain three lines written in a five-seven-five syllable pattern (for a total of seventeen syllables).

Preparation and instruction

Engage in poetry reading with your students. Model your ways of thinking about and making connections with the author's words. Model poetry writing for your students.

Information Gathering

Materials

Literature related to topics being studied in science or social studies

Possible activities

■ Students use center time to read content area material independently, with a partner, or with the center group.

■ Students use graphic organizers to help with comprehension and with the gathering and organization of content material. (See Figures 6–19 to 6–22 for examples and forms.)

Preparation and instruction

Make clear your expectations for the reading, and model the use of any graphic organizers that the students will be using.

Story Endings

Materials

Pencils and paper; a book on tape (first part of book only)

Possible activities

Students listen to the first part of a story and individually draw or write a possible ending. The real story ending is shared at the end of the week.

Preparation and instruction

Model the procedure once with the whole class before assigning it for centers.

Research Chart

Topic: Crab Apple Trees

Information from Literature	Where do they grow?	How tall do they grow?	What is the bark like?	What is the leaf like?	What are their uses?
Title: <u>Michigan Trees</u> (Wild Crab Apple)		8 meters	• thin • red-brown • scaly	• 5–10 cm • serrated	• fruit • wood for carving • ornamental
Title: <u>Audubon Field Guide</u> (Sweet Crab Apple)		9 meters		• 5–10 cm • saw-toothed	
Title:					

Figure 6–19 *Research Chart*

Sequencing

Materials

Picture cards; sentence strips; paragraph strips; comic strip cutouts; blank note cards; materials for writing and illustrating

Possible activities

▪ Students work in pairs. They use picture cards to sequence stories. Then they make up what the characters might say.

▪ Students work in pairs to put cut-apart comic strips back together. Then they read them aloud to be sure that their ordering makes sense.

▪ Students work in pairs to put cut-apart sentence (or paragraph) strips back together. Then they read them aloud to be sure that their ordering makes sense.

Feature Analysis Chart

Pets	Shelter	Food	Care	Uses	
Dog		dog food	• food and water • grooming • play	• pets • leader dogs • search and rescue	
Cat					
Horse	barn	• grass • grain • hay • salt lick	• vaccines • worming • foot care • food and water • stable care		
Goat					

Figure 6–20 *Feature Analysis Chart*

■ Students work in pairs to develop a picture or sentence-sequencing set. Limit the number of cards to three or four.

Preparation and instruction

Model general procedures for sequencing. With sentence, paragraph, and comic strips, show students how to draw clues from the text to predict what might logically come next.

Figure 6–21 *KWL Chart*

KWL Chart

Name: _____

Topic: _____

What I Know:	What I Wonder:	What I Have Learned:

Figure 6–22 *Gathering Information from Text Form*

Gathering Information from Text

Topic: _____

Question: _____

Findings:

Toy Company Play

Materials

Toys; materials for inventing toys; writing materials

Possible activities

■ Allow children to develop their own play scenarios, acting as toy makers, designers, advertisers, sellers, testers, reviewers, and any other roles of their choosing.

■ Provide numerous scrap materials and encourage each child to make a toy. Allow children to design toys on paper before using materials to construct them.

■ Bring in several toys for children to review. For example, reviewers may consider educational quality, safety, durability, appeal to children, room for creativity, stereotyping, or assumptions that the toys make about children.

■ Set up a pretend toy store.

■ Bring in several toys for children to examine. Have each child write an advertisement for a toy.

Preparation and instruction

Show students the materials available for play and discuss possible play roles.

We Design: Digging In

Materials

Any materials from the classroom may be used.

Possible activities

■ *Week 1:* Teams of students use center time to design a literacy center that will actually be used in your classroom. The activities must be designed to support children in exploring the content of a book. Activities could focus on predicting, monitoring understandings, making personal connections, visualizing, retelling, or summarizing.

■ *Weeks 2–6:* Implement one student-created center each week (or implement two per week).

■ Teams of students design a literacy center that could be used by another class in the school. The activities must be designed to support children in exploring the content of the books. Activities could focus on predicting, monitoring understandings, making personal connections, visualizing, retelling, or summarizing.

Preparation and instruction

Discuss possibilities for designing the centers. Use centers that you have designed as examples. The students may wish to replicate your designs. If other classes are to be involved, consult with the teachers of those classes. Encourage children to focus on promoting relevant comprehension goals.

Word Reading and Spelling

Special Library

Materials

Books that have been or will be used for small-group reading instruction; other books, selected to ensure that each student will be able to read them successfully

Possible activities

■ Students reread books that have been used for small-group reading instruction.

■ Students preview and read books that will be used for small-group reading instruction.

■ Students read books that you have selected for or with them and determined to be at their independent reading level (or close to it).

Preparation and instruction

Help students learn to locate books that they can read independently.

Word Puzzles and Games

Materials

Materials for writing; various word puzzles and games

Possible activities

■ Students create a word search (see Figure 6–23).

■ Students play bingo with words, pictures, or letters. Two excellent make-your-own-card sites:

www.dltk-cards.com/bingo/
www.bestteachersites.com/web_tools/materials/bingo/

■ Students play computer games from websites such as the following:

www.funschool.com
www.kidsdomain.com/games/index.html

■ Alphabet Challenge: Using each letter of the alphabet only *once*, students make a list of words, trying to use up all of the letters. All of the words together should use only twenty-six letters. (See Figure 6–24.)

■ Word Challenge: Using only the letters in the word _____ (provide a word for them to work with), students list all of the words that they can make. (See Figure 6–25.)

■ Word and Letter Challenge: Students write down the word _____ (provide a word) and then list all of the two-, three-, four-, five-, and six-letter words that they can make from its letters. (See Figure 6–26.)

■ Sentence Challenge: Students unscramble cut-up sentences. (Store each sentence in a separate envelope.)

Preparation and instruction

Model the activities with the whole class before implementing them in centers.

Alphabet Book Writing

Materials

Alphabet books to use as examples; materials for writing and illustrating

Possible activities

The following activities may be completed by individuals or center groups:

■ Write an alphabet book that contains one picture and one *letter* per page.

■ Write an alphabet book that contains one picture and one *word* per page.

Figure 6–23 *Word Search Form*

Word Search

1. Write words (one letter per box) vertically, horizontally, and diagonally.

2. Fill in the remaining boxes with letters.

Figure 6–24 *Alphabet Challenge Form*

Alphabet Challenge

Find a set of magnetic letters or letter cards. Using each letter of the alphabet only *once*, make a list of words. Play around with the words until you have managed to use up all of the letters. All of the words together should use only twenty-six letters. List the words below.

A B C D E F G H I J K L M N O P Q R S T U V W X Y Z

Figure 6–25 *Word Challenge Form*

Word Challenge

Using only the letters in the word _____, list
all of the words that you can make.

1.	11.
2.	12.
3.	13.
4.	14.
5.	15.
6.	16.
7.	17.
8.	18.
9.	19.
10.	20.

Word and Letter Challenge

Word: _____

List all of the two-, three-, four-, five-, and six-letter words that you can make from the letters in this word.

Two	Three	Four	Five	Six

▪ Write an alphabet book that contains one picture and one *sentence* per page.

▪ Write an alphabet book that connects with a social studies or science theme.

▪ Create one page for a class or group alphabet book. For class and group projects, the teacher may prepare one page per letter (by penciling in the letters on the back of twenty-six different pages) and placing all of the pages in the center so that children may choose which letters to they would like to do.

Preparation and instruction

Read several alphabet books to your students. Discuss their various features. Model by creating a few pages of the types of books you would like your students to make.

Alphabet Book Reading

Materials

Alphabet books

Possible activities

Students read a variety of alphabet books. Consider switching the theme of the alphabet books every few weeks.

Preparation and instruction

Clarify your expectations for reading the books.

Letter and Word Study

Materials

Words from the word wall written on small cards; a name card for each student; letter cards; picture cards; manipulatives such as play dough and sand

Possible activities

Based on your students' competencies, you can create dozens of letter and word study experiences. Following are a few ideas to help you get started.

▪ Have students sort a set of word or picture cards by various features:

Onsets: Students sort the words by their beginning sounds. They write down the words in columns and read them aloud. Then they add more of their own words to each column. (See Figure 6–27.)

Rimes: Students sort the words by their rimes (for example, *-ate, -ait, -at*). They write down the words in columns and read them aloud. Then they add more of their own words to each column. (See Figure 6–27.)

Number of Letters: Students sort the words into piles according to the number of letters they contain. They record the words in columns that show how many letters they contain. Then they add more of their own words to each column. (See Figure 6–27.)

Vowel Sounds: Students sort the words into piles according to the sound that their vowels make. They record the words in columns according to the sound their vowel makes. (For example, use *love, dove, done, none / cove, rove, stone, cone / move.*) Then they add more of their own words to each column. (See Figure 6–27.)

Alphabetical Order: Students place the cards in alphabetical order. Then they ask a friend to check their work.

- Students use letter cards to form student names. (Place a list of names in the center.)

- Students put together cut-apart student names. Store the letters for each name in a separate envelope that is labeled on the outside.

- Students place names or words in a pocket chart and read with a pointer.

- Students make letters or words with sand or play dough and say them aloud.

Preparation and instruction

- Model ways of forming, playing with, and sorting letters and words.

- After children engage in letter and word study, pull them together at the end of center time to discuss key patterns. For example, "What do we notice about most words spelled with the vowel-consonant-*e* pattern?" Or "What is the same about these names: *Manuel, Ariel,* and *Belle?*"

Word Hunts

Materials

Clipboards, paper, and pencils for recording findings; hunt cards

Figure 6–27 *Word Sort Chart*

Word Sort

Words sorted by: _____

(onsets, rimes, vowel sounds, number of letters, etc.)

Possible activities

Students move throughout the classroom hunting for words and writing them down on clipboards. For example:

- ■ Find five words that you can read.

- ■ Find five words to take home and read to a family member.

- ■ Find a word beginning with each letter of the alphabet.

- ■ Find five words that you would like to remember how to spell.

- ■ Find three words that start like *quack*.

- ■ Find three words that end with *-ing*.

- ■ Find five words that end with *-ed*.

- ■ Find five words in their plural form.

- ■ Find five past-tense words.

- ■ Find three compound words.

- ■ Find two words that rhyme with *fox*.

- ■ Find five contractions.

- ■ Find five words with only one or two letters.

- ■ Find three words with more than eight letters.

- ■ Find five first names.

- ■ Find the two shortest and two longest last names in our class.

- ■ Find three words that have a spelling pattern like *grape, game, have,* and *tape*. List them in columns according to the sound that the vowel makes.

- ■ Find three words that start with vowels.

Preparation and instruction

Word hunts involve children in hunting for words all over the classroom. To prepare, create a set of laminated note cards, with one hunt per card. Punch a hole in the corner of each. You can quickly pull out one to five of these to create exactly the kind of hunt desired for the center. Just fasten the cards together with a key ring. To help you get started, examples are provided here, but it is likely that you will want to create your own hunts based on the word concepts your students are currently developing. Demonstrate procedures for hunting for words around the room.

After children engage in word hunts, pull them together at the end of center time to discuss any relevant patterns. For example, "What do we notice about all of the words that begin with *q*?" Or "When we read short words like *Cox* versus long words like *Chenoweth*, what do we notice?" Or "What are the different sounds that the words ending with *-ed* make?"

We Design: Reading

Materials

Any materials from the classroom may be used.

Possible activities

- *Week 1:* Teams of students use center time to design a literacy center that will actually be used in your classroom. The activities must be designed to support children in developing their knowledge of letters, sounds, or word identification strategies. Centers may involve word puzzles, games, writing activities, or reading activities.

- *Weeks 2–6:* Implement one student-created center each week (or implement two per week).

Preparation and instruction

Discuss possibilities for designing the centers. Use centers that you have designed as examples. The students may wish to replicate your designs. Encourage children to focus on promoting word knowledge and strategies related to word identification.

Fluency

Listening

Materials

A variety of tapes containing stories, poetry, and nonfiction; matching written texts

Possible activities

- Students listen to the tapes and follow along with the words in the text. They may read aloud with the tape using a soft voice.

- After listening and following along with the words, students turn off the tape recorder and read the same text aloud in pairs.

- After listening and following along with the words, one partner reads the same text aloud, and then the other partner reads it aloud.

Preparation and instruction

Demonstrate procedures for using the equipment.

Readers Theatre

Materials

Familiar plays or readers theatre scripts; short stories (photocopied) that include a lot of dialogue

Possible activities

- Students read a play aloud. They go through a practice run and then try to read with expression. (You can support children in choosing roles. Predictable or repetitive lines will be easier to read for students who are less advanced readers.)

- As a group, students practice a script several times and then give a performance for the class after the center period.

- Students create a script based on a photocopied short story. Each speaking part should be highlighted with a different color, and the narrator part should be highlighted with yet another color.

Preparation and instruction

Read a few scripts aloud with the whole class and model any procedures that students will need to follow for creating and sharing in the reading of a script.

Audiotaping

Materials

Short blank cassette tapes, one labeled with each student's name; paper and materials for drawing and writing

Possible activities

- Students record themselves reading a poem or short story. Then, as they listen to their reading, they think about what to improve. Then they record again. Save recordings over time as a way to track their growth.

- Students chorally read a poem or short story into a tape recorder and then listen to the product. As they listen, they create an illustration on a large piece of paper. They can share the recording and the illustration with the class after center time.

- Students write a poem and then record it. Save a series of recorded poems over time to provide evidence of student growth.

- Students write a short story and then record it. Save a series of recorded stories over time to provide evidence of student growth.

- An adult takes dictation as a student tells a story or poem. Then, the adult or the student records the piece. The student then follows along with the text while listening.

Preparation and instruction

- Model the types of recording you would like your students to do.

- Model how to use the tape recorder and how to remove and store the cassettes.

Language Transcription

Materials

An adult volunteer to take transcription; paper and pencils

Possible activities

- *Week 1:* Individual students dictate a story to a scribe. The scribe supports the student in rereading the piece aloud.

- *Week 2 (optional):* Students illustrate their stories and practice reading them aloud.

Preparation and instruction

Instruct volunteers to transcribe the children's language exactly as it is stated, and ask them to encourage the children to pay attention to and participate in spelling and punctuation decisions.

Expressive Reading

Materials

Short poems; books; stories; and jokes

Possible activities

■ Students work in pairs. Each partner chooses a poem and practices reading it aloud several times. Partners give each other suggestions for how to improve.

■ Students work in pairs. Each partner finds an interesting paragraph from a book and practices reading it aloud several times. Partners give each other suggestions for how to improve.

■ Each student chooses a short book or story and prepares to read it aloud to the class (or to another class in the school). Students practice reading their books aloud several times.

■ Students work as a center group. They create a list of ten words that are fun to read expressively and practice reading them aloud to each other. For example, how might they read the words *hilarious, frightening, bored, howl, capture, weary, wriggle, chomp, crabby,* and *meow*?

■ Each student chooses a joke and practices telling it with expression.

■ Each student writes a pretend speech about something he or she cares about. Students practice reading their speeches aloud and then share them with the class after center time. (To help students understand the genre, model writing a short speech and discuss possible speech content before implementing this center. For example, you and/or students might make a case for conservation of habitats, animal rights, or limits on water pollution.)

Preparation and instruction

■ Model expressive reading for your students. Contrast this with inexpressive reading.

■ Model how to choose texts written at appropriate levels of difficulty or complexity. Texts for practicing and refining expressive reading should be relatively easy for the student to read.

Big Books

Materials

Familiar big books; a pointer; an easel; word frames; sticky notes

Possible activities

■ Students take turns reading aloud from books that have been read to the class. Listeners follow along with the print.

■ Students chorally read books aloud. One child uses a pointer.

■ While following along with the print, students listen to a peer read one line at a time and repeat after each line.

■ Students use big books to talk to and teach each other about words. They play around with framing individual words and reading them and with covering certain words with sticky notes to see if others can use the surrounding context to guess what they are.

■ After you cover some of the words in a big book with sticky notes, students read the book, making predictions about the words and checking them as they go.

Preparation and instruction

Share books with students, demonstrating the use of a pointer to track the print. Discuss possible ways of reading the books. Model using big books to learn about and study words.

News Play

Materials

Writing materials; clipboards; transparency machine; transparency sheets; dry-erase markers; news reports; weather reports; play microphones

Possible activities

■ Allow children to develop their own play scenarios, acting as weather reporters, news reporters, journalists, meteorologists, or any other roles of their choosing.

■ Assign each child to write a weather or news report. Encourage students to practice reading their reports aloud before playing as reporters.

■ Place news and weather reports in the center and encourage students to read them aloud and discuss them.

Preparation and instruction

Show students the materials available for play and discuss possible play roles.

Writing

Drafting, Revising, and Editing

Materials

Materials for composing and illustrating; reference materials as necessary; computers for word processing if available

Possible activities

The following activities can be completed by individuals:

- Write a story. Consider using a graphic organizer to help with planning. (See Figures 6–5, 6–6, and 6–7.)

- Write a poem.

- Write a nonfiction piece related to the science or social studies curriculum. Consider using a graphic organizer to help with planning. (See Figures 6–8, 6–9, 6–17, 6–19, and 6–20.)

- Write a true story or narrative about something that you have experienced.

- Draw a picture and write about it.

- Write anything you wish.

- Make a list of topics that you might like to write about. Circle your two favorites.

- Share a piece of writing with a friend. Discuss what the two of you like and what might be improved.

- Revise a piece that you have written.

- Write and illustrate one page of a class book. Start your page with one of the following:

  - I can . . .

  - I like . . .

  - I dislike . . .

  - My (mom, dad, brother, sister, grandmother, or grandfather) . . .

  - My friend . . .

- Here is what I know about _____:

- Here is what I have learned about _____:

Preparation and instruction

Model writing throughout the year. Encourage children to explore varied topics and varied genres. As appropriate to the age level and writing sophistication of your students, model techniques for revising and editing.

Publishing

Materials

Materials for writing and illustrating; reference materials as necessary; computers for word processing if available

Possible activities

Students can complete the following activities individually:

- Illustrate a written piece.

- Use the word processor to type in and print a final copy of a composition.

- Recopy a draft that has been edited and revised and then create illustrations for it.

- Create an "About the Author" page for a finished composition.

- Create an *acknowledgements* or a *dedication* page for a finished composition.

- Create a front or back cover for a finished composition.

Preparation and instruction

Model ways of putting final touches on compositions.

Note to Someone

Materials

Pencils; paper; stationery; envelopes

Possible activities

- Students write a note to a classmate.

- Students write a note to a family member.

- Students write a note to an author of a book.

- Students write a note to a public figure in the school or community.

- Students write a note to a favorite book or television character or to a famous person in history. (It might be fun to compile these notes into a class book.)

- Students write a note to a pen pal in the school district or beyond. (See *www.epals.com.*)

Preparation and instruction

Model note and envelope writing.

Message Writing

Materials

Easel and large paper or whiteboard for modeling; varied colors of markers

Possible activities

- Students (playing as teacher) take turns modeling the writing of a few sentences. If they wish, they can call on "students" to help them with words and letters, or they might wish to pretend to make errors so that the "students" can practice spotting them.

- Each group composes a few sentences to share with the class at the end of center time. The topic should be of their choosing. For example, the students might write about someone in the group getting a new puppy, moving into a new home, or losing a tooth. Or they could focus on school events, writing about something they learned in science, a book they have listened to, or their favorite activity of the morning. The group should edit the piece. Then, one of the students "teaches" the whole class by doing the writing and seeking help from the class (as teachers often do) to make decisions about spelling and punctuation.

Preparation and instruction

Model writing messages to the class, and model how to choose a topic. If you already do a daily message session with your students, then little extra modeling will be required for this center.

Observation

Materials

Content area materials that need to be observed (such as a snails, rocks and soil, floating and sinking objects, a photograph, a painting, a quilt, or a costume); materials for recording observations (pencils and journals or observation logs)

Possible activities

- Students write open-ended observations to prepare for a lesson.

- Students write questions about the materials.

- Students write predictions about what will happen or what will be learned.

- Students write for five minutes using as much descriptive language as possible and then share the writing with their group. What did most people notice? What important observations did some people miss?

Preparation and instruction

Model writing for observational purposes.

Post Office Play

Materials

Paper; envelopes; stationery; mailbox; packing materials; materials for writing and drawing

Possible activities

- Allow children to set the course for their own play.

- Require students to write at least one letter as they play.

Preparation and instruction

Discuss role possibilities with students. For example, they might wish to write letters, sort mail, deliver mail, pack and wrap packages, or play as a truck driver or mail carrier.

We Design: Writing

Materials

Any materials from the classroom may be used.

Possible activities

- *Week 1:* Teams of students use center time to design a literacy center that will actually be used in your classroom. The activities must support children in exploring some aspect of writing. Activities could focus on aspects such as choosing meaningful topics, using thoughtful vocabulary, trying a new genre, writing in a different voice, or making illustrations match with words.

- *Week 2:* Implement one student-created center each week (or implement two per week).

Preparation and instruction

Discuss possibilities for designing the centers. Use centers that you have designed as examples. The students may wish to replicate your designs. Encourage children to focus on promoting relevant writing goals.

Vocabulary

Story Sharing

Materials

Stories; story props; writing materials; story boxes

Possible activities

- Establish a story museum, in which each child displays an object from home and shares its story. Possibilities include handmade crafts, art, favorite books, recipes, poems, photographs, tools, and toys.

  Week 1: Depending on their capabilities, children write a description or create a decorated label for each object in the display.
  Week 2: Children browse the display and discuss the items.

- Students use story boxes to tell stories. Story boxes are collections of items, sometimes suggestively related, that can be used to play around with story. In an empty shoe or laundry detergent box, you might place

- three miniature dinosaurs

- ten marbles, one ring, and a few pieces of multicolored fabric

- one troll and three goats

- ten shells, a piece of blue fabric, and a piece of tan fabric

- miniature toy animals and several pipe cleaners

- paper, pencils, a stapler, scissors, Popsicle sticks, glue, and crayons

- miniature cars, long strips of paper, and tape

- three animal puppets

Preparation and instruction

Model your own storytelling. Discuss story possibilities with students.

Word Exchange

Materials

Big books; a pocket chart; pocket chart poems; sticky notes; note cards; materials for writing; pieces of student writing

Possible activities

- Students replace a specified number of words in a big book with synonyms on sticky notes. Then they read the book aloud to be sure that the text still makes sense.

- Students place the lines of a poem (or short story) in a pocket chart. They substitute a specified number of words by writing on note cards. Then they read the poem aloud to be sure that the text still makes sense.

- Students select a piece of their own writing. Working with the group, they read through it and find words that could be replaced with more interesting or descriptive words.

Preparation and instruction

Model how to do the activities. If desired, show students how to use a thesaurus.

All the Words You Can Think Of

Materials

Note cards and pencils

Possible activities

Students work collaboratively to list all the words they can think of, for example:

- for the color green

- to describe being happy, excited, mad, worried, bored, tired, energetic, hungry, full, restless, sore, or grouchy

- to use instead of *said*

- to use instead of *looked*

- to use instead of *like*

- to describe a bicycle, a cheetah, a marigold, or a friend

- with the same root or base

- with the same prefix or suffix

- snail words

- pumpkin words

- weather words

- magnet words

- shapes

- compound words

- math words

- words with more than one meaning

Write the words on note cards and place them on a key ring for future reference while students are writing.

Preparation and instruction

Choose a topic and model the process by taking suggestions from the class. To prepare for this center, create a set of laminated note cards with one activity per card. Punch a hole in the corner of each. You can quickly pull out two or three of these to create exactly the kind of activity desired for the center. Just fasten the cards together with a key ring. To help you get started, examples are provided here, but it is likely that you will want to create your own activities based on the concepts your students are currently exploring.

Vocabulary Study

Materials

Writing materials; collage materials; graphic organizers; books

Possible activities

- Students make a word collage. They write the key word in the center of a piece of paper and surround it with illustrations or pictures cut from magazines.

- Students illustrate a word to show its meaning.

- Students dramatize a word to show its meaning.

- Students sculpt a word to show its meaning.

- Students use a graphic organizer to develop insight into a word's meaning (see Figures 6–28 to 6–30 for examples).

- Students browse through a content book and find three words that are new to them. They write down the words, what they think the words mean, and how they determined the words' meanings. Then they discuss the words with the class after center time.

Preparation and instruction

Model the activities before students complete them independently.

Text Sets

Materials

Visit the school library so that children may create a text set. Focus on a theme, perhaps related to the social studies or science curriculum. (Varied texts focused on the same topic will provide several exposures to a common vocabulary.) For example, children might be encouraged to choose books

Figure 6–28 *Word Study Map*

Word Study

Word:

How the word was used in a sentence:

_____

_____

_____

Definition (in my own words):

Synonyms: _____ _____ _____

How I might use the word in a sentence that connects with what I know:

_____

_____

_____

Figure 6–29 *Connecting with Words Map*

Connecting with Words

Word:	Definition in My Own Words:

Visual Representation:

Examples:

Personal Connection:

Figure 6–30 *Exploring Word Meanings Map*

Exploring Word Meanings

Word

Synonyms

Use the word in a sentence that relates to you.

Create a visual representation of the word.

- related to bats, volcanoes, feelings, or favorite things to do

- including fun language such as onomatopoeia, idioms, homophones, or homographs

- that have creative rhymes, riddles, or jokes

Possible activities

- Students use the books for independent reading.

- Students use the books for paired reading.

Preparation and instruction

Clarify your expectations for the type of reading that you want your students to do.

Author and Book Publisher Play

Materials

Writing materials; materials for making books

Possible activities

- Students play as authors and illustrators of word-related books. They make dictionaries, picture dictionaries, thesauruses, synonym books, antonym books, riddle books, and more.

- Consider publishing a few books and donating them to other classrooms in the school.

Preparation and instruction

Discuss possible roles and activities with students.

Adams, M. 1990. *Beginning to Read: Thinking and Learning About Print*. Cambridge: MIT Press.

Allington, R. 2001. *What Really Matters for Struggling Readers: Designing Research-Based Programs*. New York: Longman.

————. 2002. "What I've Learned About Effective Reading Instruction from a Decade of Studying Exemplary Elementary Classroom Teachers." *Phi Delta Kappan* 83 (10): 740–47.

Audubon Society. 1980. *The Audubon Society Field Guide to North American Trees*. New York: Alfred A. Knopf.

Barnes, B., and W. Wagner. 1981. *Michigan Trees*. Ann Arbor: University of MI Press.

Barton, J., and D. Sawyer. 2003. "Our Students *Are* Ready for This: Comprehension Instruction in the Elementary School." *The Reading Teacher* 57 (4): 334–37.

Ben-Ari, R. 2004. "Complex Instruction and Cognitive Development." 17 July. Accessed at *www.lookstein.org/heterogeneous/Complex%20Instruction%20 and%20Cognitive%20Development%20%282a%29.htm*. Article adapted from *Working for Equity in Heterogeneous Classrooms: Sociological Theory in Practice*, ed. E. Cohen and R. Lotan. New York: Teachers College Press. 1997.

Biederman, N. 1999. "Managing Self-Directed Learning in a Multigrade Classroom." Master's thesis, Saginaw Valley State University.

Blachowicz, C., and P. Fisher. 2000. "Vocabulary Instruction." In *Handbook of Reading Research*, vol. 3, ed. M. Kamil, P. Mosenthal, P. D. Pearson, and R. Barr, 503–24. Mahwah, NJ: Lawrence Erlbaum.

Bredekamp, S., and C. Copple. 1997. *Developmentally Appropriate Practice in Early Childhood Programs*. Washington, DC: National Association for the Education of Young Children.

Brewer, J. 1992. *Early Childhood Education*. Needham Heights, MA: Allyn and Bacon.

Brown, S. 2003. "Is It Curtains for Gutta-Percha?" *Fortune* 148 (13): 58–60.

Brozo, W. 2003. "Making Word Learning Memorable." *Thinking Classrooms* 4 (4): 47–48.

Dewey, J. 1897. "My Pedagogic Creed." *School Journal* 54 (January): 77–80.

Dyson, A. 1989. *Multiple Worlds of Child Writers*. New York: Teachers College Press.

Edelsky, C. 1986. *Writing in a Bilingual Program: Habia una vez.* Norwood, NJ: Ablex.

Ferreiro, E., and A. Teberosky. 1982. *Literacy Before Schooling*. Trans. K. Castro. Portsmouth, NH: Heinemann.

Ford, M., and M. Opitz. 2002. "Using Centers to Engage Children During Guided Reading Time." *The Reading Teacher* 55 (8): 710–21.

Gavelek, J., T. Raphael, S. Biondo, and D. Wang. 2000. "Integrated Literacy Instruction." In *Handbook of Reading Research*, vol. 3, ed. M. Kamil, P. Mosenthal, P. D. Pearson, and R. Barr, 587–608. Mahwah, NJ: Lawrence Erlbaum.

Goodman, K., and Y. Goodman. 1990. "Vygotsky in a Whole Language Perspective." In *Vygotsky and Education*, ed. L. Moll, 223–50. Cambridge: Cambridge University Press.

Goodman, Y., and S. Wilde. 1992. *Literacy Events in a Community of Young Writers*. New York: Teachers College Press.

Graves, D. 1983. *Writing: Teachers and Children at Work*. Portsmouth, NH: Heinemann.

International Reading Association. 1998. *Standards for Reading Professionals*. Rev. Newark, DE: International Reading Association.

Jensen, E. 2000. *Brain-Based Learning*. San Diego, CA: Brain Store.

Johnson, J., J. Christie, and T. Yawkey. 1987. *Play and Early Childhood Development*. Glenview, IL: Scott, Foresman.

Klenk, L., and M. Kibby. 2000. "Re-mediating Reading Difficulties: Appraising the Past, Reconciling the Present, Constructing the Future." In *Handbook of Reading Research*, vol. 3, ed. M. Kamil, P. Mosenthal, P. D. Pearson, and R. Barr, 667–90. Mahwah, NJ: Lawrence Erlbaum.

Kohn, A. 1993. *Punished by Rewards: The Trouble with Gold Stars, Incentive Plans, A's, Praise, and Other Bribes*. Boston: Houghton Mifflin.

Kopacz, K. 2003. "Not Just One Teacher! Students' Development as Writers Within a Heterogeneous Group." Master's thesis, Saginaw Valley State University.

Kostelnik, M., L. Stein, A. Whiren, and A. Soderman. 1993. *Guiding Children's Social Development*. Albany, NY: Delmar.

LaBerge, D., and J. Samuels. 1974. "Toward a Theory of Automatic Information Processing in Reading." *Cognitive Psychology* 6: 293–323.

Lindfors, J. 1991. *Children's Language and Learning*. Needham Heights, MA: Allyn and Bacon.

Lowman, L., and L. Ruhmann. 1998. "Simply Sensational Spaces: A Multi-'S' Approach to Toddler Environments." *Young Children* 58 (3): 11–17.

Moll, L., and J. Greenberg. 1990. "Creating Zones of Possibilities: Combining Social Contexts for Instruction." In *Vygotsky and Education*, ed. L. Moll, 319–48. Cambridge: Cambridge University Press.

National Reading Panel. 2000. *Teaching Children to Read: An Evidenced-Based Assessment of the Scientific Research Literature on Reading and Its Implications for Reading Instruction*. Washington, DC: National Institute of Child Health and Human Development.

National Research Council. 1998. *Preventing Reading Difficulties in Young Children*. Ed. C. Snow, M. S. Burns, and P. Griffin. National Academy of Sciences.

Neuman, S., and K. Roskos. 1992. "Literacy Objects as Cultural Tools: Effects on Children's Literacy Behaviors in Play." *Reading Research Quarterly* 27 (3): 203–25.

Oakes, J., and M. Lipton. 2003. *Teaching to Change the World*. Boston: McGraw-Hill.

Ogle, D. 1986. "KWL: A Teaching Model That Develops Active Reading of Expository Text." *The Reading Teacher* 32: 564–70.

Osborn, J., F. Lehr, and E. Hiebert. 2004. "A Focus on Fluency." Product #ES0303. Pacific Resources for Education and Learning. Accessed on 21 March at *www.prel.org/products/re_/fluency-1.htm*.

Owocki, G. 2003. *Comprehension: Strategic Instruction for K–3 Students*. Portsmouth, NH: Heinemann.

Owocki, G., and Y. Goodman. 2002. *Kidwatching: Documenting Children's Literacy Development*. Portsmouth, NH: Heinemann.

Piaget, J. 1952. *The Construction of Reality in the Child*. New York: Basic.

Petrakos, H., and N. Howe. 1996. "The Influence of the Physical Design of the Dramatic Play Center on Children's Play." *Early Childhood Research Quarterly* 11 (1). Accessed at *www.udel.edu/ECRQ/sum1112.html*.

Pressley, M. 2000. "What Should Comprehension Instruction Be the Instruction Of?" In *Handbook of Reading Research*, vol. 3, ed. M. Kamil, P. Mosenthal, P. D. Pearson, and R. Barr, 545–62. Mahwah, NJ: Lawrence Erlbaum.

Pressley, M., R. Allington, R. Wharton-McDonald, C. Block, and L. Morrow. 2001. *Learning to Read: Lessons from Exemplary First Grade Classrooms.* New York: Guilford.

Pressley, M., J. Rankin, and L. Yokoi. 2000. "A Survey of Instructional Practices of Primary Teachers Nominated as Effective in Promoting Literacy." In *Issues and Trends in Literacy Education*, 2d ed., ed. R. Robinson, M. McKenna, and J. Wedman, 10–34. Needham Heights, MA: Allyn and Bacon.

Rasinski, T. 2004. "Creating Fluent Readers." *Educational Leadership* 61 (6): 46–51.

Roskos, K. 1995. "Creating Places for Play with Print." In *Readings for Linking Literacy and Play*, 8–17. Newark, DE: International Reading Association.

Schickedanz, J. 1999. *Much More Than the ABCs*. Washington, DC: National Association for the Education of Young Children.

Slavin, R. 1987. *Ability Grouping and Student Achievement in Elementary School: A Best Evidence Synthesis*. Baltimore, MD: Center for Research on Elementary and Secondary Schools, John Hopkins University.

Taylor, B. M., P. D. Pearson, K. Clark, and S. Walpole. 2000. "Effective Schools and Accomplished Teachers: Lessons About Primary-Grade Reading Instruction in Low-Income Schools." *Elementary School Journal* 101 (2): 121–65.

Thoreau, H. [1855–1861] 1984. *The Journal of Henry David Thoreau*. 14 vols. Salt Lake City, UT: Peregrine Smith.

Vygotsky, L. 1978. *Mind in Society: The Development of Higher Psychological Processes*. Ed. and trans. M. Cole, V. John-Steiner, S. Scribner, and E. Souberman. Cambridge: Harvard University Press.

Whitmore, K., P. Martens, Y. Goodman, and G. Owocki. 2004. "Critical Lessons from the Transactional Perspective on Early Literacy Research." *Journal of Early Childhood Literacy* 4 (3): 291–325.

Activities
    collaborative, 37
    discussing, 63–64
    effective literacy instruction from
        variety of, 8–9
    modeling, 63–64
    with on-the-spot differentiation, 71,
        72–73
    with structured differentiation,
        72–73, 74–76
All the Words You Can Think Of
    center, 90, 147–48
Alphabet Book Reading center, 89, 132
Alphabet Book Writing center, 89, 127,
    132
Alphabet Challenge, 127, 129
Alphabet knowledge, as goal for
    centers, 22–23
Assessment
    adjusting instruction based on, 9
    of center environments, 43, 45
    center time assessment, 78, 80–87
    fiction, evaluating, 113, 115
    individual learning progress, 7–9
    from interest perspective, 6
    long-term monitoring, 79
    observation of students and center
        activities, 62–63
Audiotaping center, 89, 137–38
Author and Book Publisher Play center,
    90, 152

Behavior, setting goals for, 64–66, 67
Ben-Ari, R., 47

Big Books center, 89, 139–40
Bilingual learners, context with, 30
Bingo, 127
Book areas, 38–39
Book Discussion center, 89, 100
Book-Handling and -Sharing centers,
    89, 98–104
    Book Discussion, 89, 100
    Book Making, 89, 101
    Book Talks, 89, 101–103
    Listen and Share, 89, 98–99
    Partner Reading, 89, 99–100
    Teacher Play, 89, 104
Book-handling competencies, 19–20
Book Making center, 89, 101
Book-sharing competencies, 19–20
Book Talks center, 89, 101–103
Boundaries, center, 33–35
Bredekamp, Susan, 15
Brozo, William, 29
Bush, Christian, 5–7, 69–71, 74

Center ideas, 88–152
Centers, literacy. See Literacy centers
Children's role in differentiated
    instruction, 78
Choice, in centers, 37
Clutter, in centers, 41
Collaborative activities, 37
Comprehension and Meaning-Making
    centers, 89, 104–26
    Drama and Retelling, 89, 105,
        106–10
    as goal for centers, 20–22

Comprehension and Meaning-Making centers (*cont.*)
    Information Gathering, 89, 120–24
    Literature Response, 89, 105, 113–14, 115–19
    Poetry, 89, 114, 120
    Reading, 89, 104
    Sequencing, 89, 121–22
    Story Endings, 89, 120
    Toy Company Play, 89, 125
    We Design: Digging In, 89, 125–26
Conduct, setting goals for, 64–66, 67
Copple, Carol, 15

Dewey, John, 7, 8
Differentiated instruction, 69–87
    assessment, center time, 78, 80–87
    characteristics, 70–78
    child's role, 78
    long-term monitoring, 79
    on-the-spot differentiation, 70–74
    structured differentiation, 74–77
Differentiation, 2–3, 8
    with alphabet knowledge, 23
    with bilingual or English language learners, 30
    in book-handling and -sharing, 20
    center books, 39
    choice and, 37
    collaboration, center, 48
    with comprehension strategies, 22
    with fluency, 27
    folders, 42
    grouping students, 42
    letters and sounds, developing, 24
    and literacy goals, 17
    materials in center, student-input on preferences for, 35
    neatness, 41
    planning period, use of, 49
    plans, small-group minilesson on, 51
    play, 40
    private spaces and, 38
    quiet zones, 36
    schedule boards, 43, 44
    small group *versus* whole class instruction, 64
    sociocultural practices and, 18
    special needs, revising activities for, 51
    support, working with children needing extra, 62
    teacher activities, 48
    with text-processing strategies, 26

writing, motivation for, 29
Drafting, Revising, and Editing center, 89, 141–42
Drama and Retelling center, 89, 105, 106–10
Drawings
    book talks with, 101, 102
    of plans for the day, 51, 52

Editing, center, 141–42
English language learners, context with, 30
Environments for centers, physical. *See* Physical environments
Evaluation. *See* Assessment
Expectations, establishing clear, 55, 62
Expressive Reading center, 89, 138–39

Family connections, 18
Family Design center, 89, 97–98
Family Literacy center, 88, 93–94
Family Literacy Materials center, 88, 93
Family Recording form, 91, 92
Family Tales center, 88, 90–91
Feature Analysis Chart for information gathering center, 120, 122
Fiction, evaluating, 113, 115
Fixed areas, classroom, 33
Fluency, as goal for centers, 27
Fluency centers, 89, 136–40
    Audiotaping, 89, 137–38
    Big Books, 89, 139–40
    Expressive Reading, 89, 138–39
    Language Transcription, 89, 138
    Listening, 89, 136–37
    News Play, 89, 140
    Readers Theatre, 89, 137
Ford, Michael P., 16

Games and Puzzles centers, 89, 126–27, 128–31
Gavelek, J., 11
Goals, literacy, 16–30
    alphabet knowledge, 22–23
    book-handling and -sharing competencies, 19–20
    comprehension strategies, 20–22
    language and literacy as sociocultural practices, 17–18
    list of, 17
    phonological awareness and phonics knowledge, 23–24
    reading fluency, 27

text-processing strategies, 24–26
vocabulary, 29–30
word knowledge, 24, 25
word reading and spelling, 22–26
writing, uses of and knowledge
about, 27–29
Goals, setting behavior, 64–66, 67
Graphic organizers, 64
Greeting Cards center, 89, 96–97
Group-in-one-center rotation model,
49, 51, 54, 56–57
Group with choice rotation model, 49,
55, 58–61

Haiku, 120
Handwriting, as goal for centers, 18
Heterogeneous groups, 47
Homework Talk center, 88, 95–96
Hush zones, 31, 36

Illustrations
book talks with, 101, 102
plans for the day, 51, 52
Individual pace rotation model, 48–51,
52–54
Information Gathering center, 89,
120–24
Information webs, 105, 110
Ingle, Marie, 1–4, 6
Instructional support
with on-the-spot differentiation,
70–71, 72
with structured differentiation, 72, 74
Instruction cards, 43, 44
Interests, meaningful learning from
student, 5–7
International Reading Association, 11,
16

Job Play center, 89, 97

Kid Tales center, 88, 91, 93
KWL Chart, 120, 123

Language, as sociocultural practice,
17–18
Language arts, defined, 11
Language Transcription center, 89, 138
Learning
environments, 14–15
optimal time for, 66
Learning, meaningful. *See* Meaningful
learning

Learning principles, 2–15
individual learning progress, 7–9
interests, tastes and preferences,
5–7
meaningful and functional activity,
10–13
sociocultural experiences, 3–5
talk and social collaboration, 9–10
teacher within, 14–15
Letter and Word Study center, 89,
132–33, 134
Letter-of-the-week programs, 24
Lipton, Martin, 5
Listen and Share center, 89, 98–99
Listening center, 89, 136–37
Literacy
activities, effective instruction from
variety of, 8–9
progress, characteristics of, 7–8
as sociocultural practice, 17–18
talk, from knowledge-enhancing, 10
Literacy centers
learning principles and (*see* Learning
principles)
physical environments for (*See*
Physical environments)
as places for all learners, 1–2
planning form for, 11–13
Literacy goals. *See* Goals, literacy
Literature, evaluating, 113, 115
Literature Response center, 89, 105,
113–14, 115–19
Logistics
with on-the-spot differentiation, 71,
73, 74
with structured differentiation, 73,
76–77

Management, center, 46–68
behavior, setting goals for, 64–66,
67
grouping students, 47–48
group-in-one-center rotation model,
49, 51, 54, 56–57
group with choice rotation model,
49, 55, 58–61
individual pace rotation model,
48–51, 52–54
models for rotation, selecting, 47–55,
56–57
observing, 62–63
optimal time to learn and teach, 66
routines, establishing clear, 55, 62

Management, center (*cont.*)
  routines and activities, smooth
      running of, 55, 62–66
  teachers, role of, 48
  transitions, working with, 66, 68
Materials for centers
  clutter, avoiding, 41
  with on-the-spot differentiation, 71,
      72–73
  selecting, 36–40
  with structured differentiation,
      72–73, 74–76
  supplying the proper amount of, 41,
      42
Meaningful learning, 2–3
  individual learning progress in, 7–9
  from interests, tastes and preferences,
      5–7
  from meaningful and functional
      activity, 10–13
  from sociocultural experiences, 3–5
  from talk and social collaboration,
      9–10
  from teacher within, 14–15
Meaning-making centers. *See*
      Comprehension and meaning-
      making centers
Message Writing center, 89, 143
Miscue analysis, 26
Modeling, activities, 63–64
Motivation, in new language learning, 6
Movement, in center design, 40–41

National Association for the Education
      of Young Children, 16
National Council of Teachers of
      English, 16
Neatness, in centers, 41
News Play center, 89, 140
Nonfiction, evaluating, 113, 115
Note to Someone center, 89, 142–43

Oakes, Jeannie, 5
Observation
  reading aloud, 78, 90
  retelling, 78, 82
  of students and center activities, 62–63
  writing, 78, 85
Observation center, 90, 144
On-the-spot differentiation, 70–74
Opitz, Michael F., 16
Oral reading, organizing instruction
      based on, 81

Parents, family literacy letter to, 93–94
Partner Reading center, 89, 99–100
Phonics knowledge
  as goal for centers, 18, 23–24
  key concepts, 24, 25
Phonological awareness
  as goal for centers, 23–24
  key concepts, 24, 25
Physical environments, 31–45
  ability to work, considering
      children's, 40–43
  arrangement, 34
  assessment of, 43
  book areas, 38–39
  boundaries, 33–35
  clutter, 41
  collaborative activities, 37
  fixed areas, 33
  instruction cards, 43, 44
  layout, 33–35
  movement, 40–41
  neatness, 41
  numbers of students in center, 42
  private spaces, 37–38
  props and materials, selecting,
      36–40
  safety, 40
  schedule boards, 43, 44
  small-group teaching area, 36
  sociodramatic play areas, 39–40
  soft areas, 38
  space, creating, 32–33, 34
  traffic, 35–36
  work, finished and unfinished, 42
Pictures
  book talks with, 101, 102
  plans for the day, 51, 52
Planning
  for differentiated instruction, 66, 67
  form for literacy centers, 11–13
  plans for the day, 51, 52
  plans for the week, 51, 53
Play areas, sociodramatic, 39–40
Poetry center, 89, 114, 120
Post Office Play center, 90, 144
Preferences, meaningful learning from
      student, 5–7
Pressley, M., 8–9
Private spaces, 37–38
Props for centers, selecting, 36–40
Publishing center, 89, 142
Puzzles and Games centers, 89, 126–27,
      128–31

Quiet zones, 31, 36

Readers Theatre center, 89, 137
Reading
  assessment, 80–84
  beginning, 23
  expressive, 138–39
  fluency, as goal for centers, 27
  long-term monitoring of growth,
    79
  real, 17–18
  small-group instruction,
    differentiating, 75
  word reading and spelling, as goal for
    centers, 22–26
  word reading and spelling centers (see
    Word reading and spelling
    centers)
Reading aloud
  observation, 78, 90
  organizing instruction based on, 81
Reading center, 89, 104
Reading centers activities, examples of,
    54–55
Reading the room, 31–32
Recreation center, 88, 95
Reproducibles
  Alphabet Challenge, 127, 129
  Book Talk Picture Form, 101, 102
  Book Talk Writing Form, 101, 103
  Character/Personality Connections
    Map, 113, 116
  Connecting with Words Map, 148,
    150
  Connections Between Texts Map,
    113, 119
  Detailed Story Map, 105, 108
  Evaluation of Center Environment,
    43, 45
  Exploring Word Meanings Map, 148,
    151
  Family Literacy: Letter to Parents, 93,
    94
  Feature Analysis Chart, 120, 122
  Fiction Evaluation Form, 113, 115
  Framework for Family Recording,
    91, 92
  Gathering Information from Text,
    120, 124
  General Story Map, 105, 107
  Goals (conduct), 64, 65
  Group-in-One-Center Model, 55,
    56–57

Group-in-One-Center Model 1, 55,
    58–59
Group-in-One-Center Model 2, 55,
    59
Group-in-One-Center Model 3, 55,
    60
Information Web, 105, 110
Informational Text Map, 105, 109
  KWL Chart, 120, 123
  Nonfiction Evaluation Form, 113,
    115
  Organizing Differentiated Instruction
    Based on Read-Alouds, 78, 81
  Organizing Differentiated Instruction
    Based on Retellings, 78, 83
  Organizing Differentiated Instruction
    Based on Writing, 78, 86
  Organizing for Differentiated
    Instruction Planning Form, 66,
    67
  Planning Forms for Literacy centers,
    11, 12–13
  Read-Aloud Observation, 78, 80
  Research Chart, 120, 121
  Retelling Informational Texts, 105,
    112
  Retelling Observation, 78, 82
  Retelling Stories, 105, 111
  Story Sequencing Map, 105, 106
  Three-Column Comparison Chart,
    113, 117
  Venn Diagram, 113, 118
  Word and Letter Challenge, 127, 131
  Word Challenge, 127, 130
  Word Search, 127, 128
  Word Sort Chart, 133, 134
  Word Study Map, 148, 149
  Write or Draw Plans for the Day, 51,
    52
  Write Plans for the Week, 51, 53
  Writing Conference: Possible
    Directions, 78, 86
  Writing Observation, 78, 85
Research chart for information
    gathering center, 120, 121
Retelling, 82–84
  Drama and Retelling center, 89, 105,
    106–10
  observation, 78, 82
Rewards, use of, 66
Rotation models
  group-in-one-center model, 49, 51,
    54, 56–57

Rotation models (*cont.*)
   group with choice model, 49, 55,
      58–61
   individual pace model, 48–51, 52–54
Routines, establishing clear, 55, 62

Safety, in centers, 40
Schedule boards, 43, 44
Schickedanz, Judith A., 39
Self-talk, meaningful learning from,
      9–10
Sentence Challenge, 127
Sequencing center, 89, 121–22
Sight word vocabulary, 24
Small-group teaching area, 36
Social collaboration, meaningful
      learning from, 9–10
Sociocultural experiences, 3–5, 79
Sociocultural Practice centers, 90–98
   Family Design, 89, 97–98
   Family Literacy, 88, 93–94
   Family Literacy Materials, 88, 93
   Family Tales, 88, 90–91
   Greeting Cards, 89, 96–97
   Homework Talk, 88, 95–96
   Job Play, 89, 97
   Kid Tales, 88, 91, 93
   Recreation, 88, 95
Sociocultural theories of learning, 5
Sociodramatic play areas, 39–40
Soft areas, in centers, 38
Space for centers, creating, 32–33, 34
Special Library center, 89, 126
Spelling
   as goal for centers, 22–26
   word reading and spelling centers (*see*
      Word reading and spelling
      centers)
Story Endings center, 89, 120
Story mapping, 105, 106–109
Story Sharing center, 90, 145–46
Structured differentiation, 74–77
Student's role in differentiated
      instruction, 78

Talk
   meaningful learning from child-
      directed, 9–10
   real, 17–18
Tastes, meaningful learning from
      student, 5–7
Teacher Play center, 89, 104
Teachers, role of, 48

Teacher within, meaningful learning
      from, 14–15
Teaching, optimal time for, 66
Tension, in new language learning, 6
Text-processing strategies, as goal for
      centers, 24–26
Texts, for fluency instruction, 27
Text Sets center, 90, 148, 152
Three Little Pigs, The, 9
Toy Company Play center, 89, 125
Traffic patterns, center, 35–36
Transitions, working with, 66, 68

Venn Diagrams, 113, 118
Vocabulary,
   as goal for centers, 29–30
   sight word, 24
Vocabulary centers, 90, 145–52
   All the Words You Can Think Of,
      90, 147–48
   Author and Book Publisher Play, 90,
      152
   Story Sharing, 90, 145–46
   Text Sets, 90, 148, 152
   Vocabulary Study, 90, 148, 149–50
   Word Exchange, 90, 146
Vocabulary Study center, 90, 148,
      149–50
Vygotsky, Lev, 11

Weather center, 69
We Design: Digging In center, 89,
      125–26
We Design: Reading center, 89, 136
We Design: Writing center, 90, 145
Word and Letter Challenge, 127, 131
Word Challenge, 127, 130
Word Exchange center, 90, 146
Word Hunts center, 89, 133, 135–36
Word knowledge, key concepts, 24, 25
Word Puzzles and Games centers, 89,
      126–27, 128–31
Word reading, as goal for centers, 22–26
Word Reading and Spelling centers, 89,
      126–36
   Alphabet Book Reading, 89, 132
   Alphabet Book Writing, 89, 127,
      132
   Letter and Word Study, 89, 132–33,
      134
   Special Library, 89, 126
   We Design: Reading, 89, 136
   Word Hunts, 89, 133, 135–36

Word Puzzles and Games, 89,
    126–27, 128–31
Word Search, 127, 128
Word Sort Chart, 133, 134
Word Study Map, 148, 149
Work, organizing places for finished
    and unfinished, 42
Writing
    alphabet book center, 89, 132
    assessment, 85–87
    beginning, 23
    with book talks, 101, 103
    competencies, 28
    long-term monitoring of growth, 79
    observation, 78, 85
    plans for the day, 51, 52
    real, 17–18
    uses of and knowledge about, as
        goals for centers, 27–29
Writing centers, 89–90, 141–45
    Drafting, Revising, and Editing, 89,
        141–42
    Message Writing, 89, 143
    Note to Someone, 89, 142–43
    Observation, 90, 144
    Post Office Play, 90, 144
    Publishing, 89, 142
    We Design: Writing, 90, 145